DREAMSPEAK

*How to Understand the Messages
in Your Dreams*

Rosemary Ellen Guiley

B
BERKLEY BOOKS, NEW YORK

A Berkley Book
Published by The Berkley Publishing Group
A division of Penguin Putnam Inc.
375 Hudson Street
New York, New York 10014

This book is an original publication of The Berkley Publishing Group.

Copyright © 2001 by Visionary Living, Inc.
Text design by Tiffany Kukec.

PRINTING HISTORY
Berkley trade paperback edition / August 2001

Visit our website at
www.penguinputnam.com

Library of Congress Cataloging-in-Publication Data

Guiley, Rosemary.
    Dreamspeak : how to understand the messages in your dreams / Rosemary Ellen Guiley.
        p. cm.
    Includes bibliographical references.
    ISBN 0-425-18142-1
    1. Dreams.   I. Title.

BF1091. G827 2001
154.6'3—dc21

2001035976

PRINTED IN THE UNITED STATES OF AMERICA

10 9 8 7 6 5 4 3 2 1

ACKNOWLEDGMENTS

I would like to thank the many individuals who contributed their dreams to this book. A special thanks of appreciation goes to my dream group partners, Sheryl Martin, O.M.D., Anne Dorsey, and Teresa Wonnell, for their invaluable help in illuminating my own dreamwork.

CONTENTS

Injured Animals · Part-Human Animals · Animals with Spiritual Messages · Magical, Mythical and Supernatural Animals

Houses and Homes · *New House* · *House in Disrepair* · *House on Fire* · *Old Homes* · *Houses That Represent Change* · *Hotels* · Buildings and Other Structures · *Tall Buildings and Towers* · *Public Buildings*

Automobiles, Difficult Roads and Getting Lost · Airplanes · Boats and Ships · Trains, Buses and Mass Transport · Streets and Traffic

Water · Earth · Fire · Air

Pursuit · Violence · Dying and Death · *Destructive Relationships* · *Dying or Dead Relationships* · *Need for Change* · Premonitory Death Dreams

How and Why the Dead Appear in Dreams · Types of Encounter Dreams · Information About Dying · Seeing the Other Side

INTRODUCTION

One of your greatest allies in life is your dreams. Whatever you seek to be, do, or accomplish, your dreams can help you in reaching your goals.

Dreams have meaning, and when we pay attention to dreams their meaning bursts upon us in profound insights. Like many people who explore the dreamworld, I have experienced these truths about dreams myself. I have been interested in dreams and have studied them for most of my life, and have learned a great deal about myself and even the "meaning of life" through the nightly panorama of dreams. Dreams have validated my intuition, saved me from unnecessary stress, presented solutions to problems, inspired me with creativity, helped to keep me "on course," and illumined my questing into the spiritual side of life. Life hasn't been perfect by any means, but dreams have contributed greatly to the establishment and maintenance of my well-being.

As long as human beings have dreamed, we have pondered the purpose and meaning of dreams. There are numerous ways to approach understanding dreams. Dreams emerge from our depths and communicate our inner truths in symbols. The more we understand the language of symbols, the more we understand our dreams. Symbols in dreams always have personal meanings related to the dreamer's context of life, but also can have a broad, more universal meaning common to many situations.

This book covers some of the most common dream symbols and themes and what they have meant in a wide variety of real-life situations. These examples are intended to serve as inspirations to spark ideas about what your own dreams mean. You, the dreamer, are the final authority in knowing your dreams.

Modern dreamwork developed from clinical psychotherapy. Today dreamwork is done within both therapeutical and lay settings. My own background is in lay dreamwork, and since the 1980s I have been active in group and individual lay dreamwork outside of therapeutical settings.

The more I explore dreams, the more I am intrigued by them—not only my own, but also the moving and power-filled dreams of others. Our dreams show not just our own inner beings, they reveal the heart of humanity as a whole. Our dreams are not just about daily life, but also about the Great Mystery. To look into dreams opens windows to the soul.

—Rosemary Ellen Guiley, Ph.D.

The Marvelous Meaning of Dreams

"I have the strangest dreams—I'd love to know what they mean!"

That's the sort of comment I hear when people discover that I'm involved in dreamwork. Our dreams do fascinate us, and they often seem so strange that we are certain others might think us peculiar if we talked about them. But when we talk about our dreams, we quickly discover that other people have dreams similar to ours. Certainly a dream is unique to the dreamer, but people share common themes and motifs that address life situations. And when we talk about our dreams we also discover that dreams are not beyond reach, but are surprisingly easy to understand.

Our dreams are not meaningless or random. They contain tremendous wisdom, and they appear in our theater of the night with purpose. Dreams provide a barometer of our emotions, help us deal with our anxieties, face our fears, validate our intuition, solve our problems and fuel our aspirations and ambitions. Dreams help us heal and grow.

Despite the proliferation of dream guidebooks today, many people don't examine their dreams, perhaps because they haven't learned the language that dreams speak. Dreamwork is important, not just for personal benefit, but for the benefit of the soul. The more we awaken to our dreams, the more we progress in life. We have improved opportunities for making life more satisfying on all levels of being.

Historical Overview

The power and importance of dreams has been recognized since ancient times. Dreams were considered a divine gift and a connection to higher realms. Dreams were consulted for important matters of state, to see into the future, and to facilitate healing. Professional dream interpreters were consulted, and pilgrims around the world visited sacred places and temples to incubate specific dreams for guidance and healing.

In the West, dreams lost their importance as science gained prominence, but the emergence of psychotherapy in the late nineteenth century turned new attention on dreams as a significant window into the interior of the psyche. Sigmund Freud saw in dreams fulfillments of repressed infantile and sexual desires. Events during the day, which Freud called "day residues," triggered nocturnal releases of these repressed elements in the form of dreams. Freud saw limited value in dreams, but his pupil Carl G. Jung plunged fully into the dreamworld and explored other dimensions that relate to the purpose and meaning of life.

Dreams, said Jung, are the expression of the contents of the personal unconscious (what pertains specifically to the individual) and the collective unconscious (what pertains to large groups of people, racially or culturally, or to humanity as a whole). The purpose of dreams is compensatory. They provide information about the self, help achieve psychic equilibrium, or offer guidance. Dreams speak in symbols. Some symbols come from the collective unconscious, which holds a reservoir of thought and behavior patterns shared by all people and is built up through time. These symbols have universal, or archetypal, meanings. For example, a personal mother symbol relates to the dreamer's own relationship and experiences, and an archetypal mother symbol contains all the positive and negative associations with the meaning of *Mother*.

Jung also observed that dreams are alchemical, that is, they are related to the process of inner transformation. Alchemy is an ancient and universal spiritual art or science. The stereotype of alchemy is that of the mad scientist trying to turn lead into gold. Alchemists of yore did search for the secrets of metals transformation, but the true pursuit of alchemy is an inner one, comparable to Jung's process of individuation. You start with yourself and all your "impurities" of flaws and shortcomings, and through experience, wisdom and insight purify yourself into a higher state of consciousness: a balanced wholeness. For Jung, dreams were especially alchemical, revealing to us the inner processes of our change, and showing us how to keep making progress.

Since Freud and Jung, others have added their own perspectives on the nature, function and meaning of dreams. Science also has contributed much to our understanding of the process of dreaming and to analyses of the contents of dreams. Since about the 1970s, dreamwork as a lay pursuit outside of psychoanalysis has become increasingly popular. Sometimes it is best to work with dreams with a therapist or counselor, but most people can gain a greater understanding of themselves by studying their dreams on their own or in the company of dreamwork groups.

Benefits of Understanding Your Dreams

You don't have to study dreams for a long time before you can get insight from them. Dreamwork is amazingly productive. The more you do it, the more rewarding it becomes as your understanding of your dreams deepens. Study does help. Reading about dream techniques and how others have interpreted their dreams will give you insights into your own dreams. Our dreams are unique to us, but they contain common threads that unite us to all others.

The high purpose of dreams is to help us to find the meaning in life. All of our experiences, good and bad, have a purpose that contributes to life meaning. Without having a sense of life meaning, happiness and fulfillment elude us. Happiness is not just having good experiences in life. Both good and bad experiences continue—it's our response to them and how we integrate them into our meaning of life that makes the difference in happiness and fulfillment.

The meaning of life changes as we age and grow in wisdom and experience. Our dreams are a vital source of energy and renewal.

Here are answers to the most frequently asked questions about dreams:

What are the most common dreams?

Certain themes occur frequently across the general population. They have acquired an archetypal significance that has a consistent meaning for many dreamers.

Probably the three most common dreams are flying, falling, and losing your teeth. Flying dreams usually are pleasant, even exhilarating. They may express a release of creative energy, or address escape issues. Falling and losing teeth are anxiety dreams. Teeth often have to do with our personal power and control.

Other common dream themes are: being nude or partially nude in public; being pursued or attacked by a monster or threatening person; being late and getting lost; losing money and valuables; being unprepared for a test or examination; driving or riding in a car, especially when the road abruptly changes to something unexpected; missing a train, plane or boat; urinating and defecating; and having sexual encounters, often with persons with whom you would never have sex in waking life.

Most dreams deal with our anxieties and fears. We worry about our ability to perform sexually and on the job; how we are regarded by other people; our self-esteem; where we are going in life; and how we are able to influence and control what happens to us. Dreams also help us address old wounds and face matters that are adversely affecting us. If we are pursued, something is demanding our attention. If we are late or lost, or on suddenly bumpy terrain, perhaps we need to reexamine what we are doing and where we are going. If we lose valuables, perhaps our priorities need changing.

These and other frequently dreamed themes will be discussed in more detail throughout this book.

Why do dreams communicate in symbols?

Although all of our senses are engaged in dreams, dreams are primarily a visual medium. Their messages are conveyed in symbols, which often seem mysterious and hard to understand. Dreamwork is simply a matter of understanding the language of dreams. The language itself is not mysterious, but very plain, and packed with information.

Pictures, images and symbols convey far more information than words. They reach us on an intuitive level that goes much deeper than written language. Pictures address emotions and experience. They engage us on all levels of our being, not just the rational mind.

Dream images reach into our hopes, fears, memories and ambitions. Our dream images relate primarily to our own personal life, but they also draw upon a collective pool of experience passed down through the ages by all of humanity.

We can understand images by making associations with them. What do they remind us of? What emotions do they invoke? How do they fit what is going on in our life?

A plan for working with dreams is presented in chapter 2.

Do we dream every night?

Scientific research indicates that, with few exceptions, we all dream every night. Some people who have suffered trauma to the brain or who have brain illness are known to experience a loss of dreaming. Otherwise, we dream throughout the night, in both rapid-eye movement (REM) sleep and non-REM periods of sleep. It was once thought that dreaming always occurred as a function of REM sleep, but research has shown that dreaming and REM are separate functions of the brain.

If we dream every night, why do I not always remember a dream when I wake up?

Some people seem to have a natural ability to remember their dreams in vivid detail, while others struggle to recall them. Stress, food, medication and stimulants can affect sleep patterns, thus potentially disrupting dream time. Dreams are very responsive, however. Simply setting your intention to remember dreams can improve your recall ability.

It's important to record dreams as soon as possible upon awakening, for they are very easy to forget. Chemicals in the brain that are related to short-term memory decrease during sleep, which may be why dreams evaporate so easily. When we awaken, we must set dreams in memory by recording them or retelling them.

Does everyone dream in color?

Most people—an estimated 75 percent of the adult population—dream in color. A higher percentage of women dream in color than men. It's not unusual to dream primarily in color and also occasionally have black-and-white dreams, which would be significant in a symbolic way. Emotions in a dream can intensify colors. Lucid dreams—being aware of dreaming during the dream—also have unusual or intense colors.

How long do dreams last?

Some do seem to go on all night! Most are short, ranging from a half minute or so to several minutes in length. REM stages, when a lot of dreaming occurs, progressively lengthen throughout the night, and can be as long as twenty to forty-five minutes. Lengths vary according to age and individual factors.

Do men and women dream differently?

Women's dreams contain more dialogue, social interaction, emotion and detail. Women's dreams are set indoors more than men's dreams, which are set more outdoors. Men's dreams contain more action and more male figures, and less dialogue.

Do dreams change as we age?

Our sleep patterns change as we age. We spend much more time in REM sleep when we are young. Dream recall decreases with age. Our dreams reflect our emotional concerns, which change in different stages of life. As we enter and go through middle age, we are likely to have more "big" dreams, that is, dreams filled with archetypal images and transcendent meanings. Such dreams can have a powerful impact on what we do with ourselves, and the decisions we make about career and relationships, and our outlook on life.

Why do so many dreams seem troublesome rather than happy?

Studies show that about two-thirds of our dreams are unpleasant or negative. Dreams are a source of intuitive guidance for our best interests and healing. They prompt us to act when life gets out of balance. Stresses, anxieties, founded and unfounded fears, self-doubts and repressed feelings all need to be healed. Dreams are helpful in that they bring imbalances to our attention.

Why do some dreams repeat?

Dreams call our attention to something we need to change, and repeat until we do so. Sometimes the very same dream repeats; more often, a theme repeats. Sometimes repeating dreams are nightmarish to the dreamer. Resolving the issue usually brings an end to the repetition.

Are nightmares different from "ordinary dreams"?

Any dream that is distressing to the dreamer can be called a nightmare. Common nightmares involve falling, being attacked or pursued, or having your teeth fall out. Everyone has a nightmare now and then. It may be the dream's way of urgently getting your attention.

Some nightmares are caused by psychological problems and post-traumatic stress disorder (PTSD). Many recurring PTSD dreams reenact a horrific event, sometimes with the twist of a worse ending. Over time, such dreams may become more metaphoric and symbolic of other concerns in life. Other nightmares may contain repressed memories about abuse or negative events. Nightmares related to PTSD, abuse and dissociative disorders are best dealt with in therapy.

Do the blind dream?

Blind people dream, but not necessarily with visual imagery. According to studies, if someone is born blind or sight is lost before age five, visual imagery is absent. Instead dream content includes the other senses, primarily hearing, as well as emotional tones. If sight is lost between ages five and seven, there may be some visual imagery. Visual imagery often is retained in dreams if sight is lost after age seven, but gradually decreases with age.

Do animals dream?

The answer to that isn't known. Animals are observed to have REM sleep, and to twitch and make noises during sleep. Throughout history, human beings have thought animals to dream. The Greek philosopher Aristotle and the Roman historian Pliny believed so, and much later Charles Darwin credited dogs, cats, horses and the "higher animals" with the ability to dream.

What is a lucid dream?

A lucid dream involves knowing you're dreaming while you're dreaming. In some cases, you can direct the events and outcome of the dream. It's estimated that about 15 percent of the adult population have frequent lucid dreams. For some of us, they are few and far between. Research has shown, however, that it is possible to teach yourself how to increase your lucid dreaming, with more lucid dreams, longer lucidity, and more control. Lucid dreaming has been linked to enhanced creativity and self-healing.

Do we go out of body when we dream?

No one knows where consciousness "goes" during sleep and dreaming—or where it "goes" when we're awake, either. We understand very little about the nature and functions of consciousness and where it "is." However, since ancient times dreams have been regarded as a place where human awareness can meet spiritual beings and the dead, as well as have real experiences. Barriers and limitations imposed by the rational mind fall away during sleep, and we are free to travel through time and space. Some dreams can be intensely spiritual in nature—we feel we are in the presence of spiritual beings or the Divine, and in other-worldly places. These can be symbolic images, or, according to ancient wisdom, real events.

How common are psychic dreams?

People probably have more psychic dreams than they realize, simply because they don't pay attention or discuss them with others. Usually we hear about psychic dreams only when they're dramatic and involve a distressing or tragic event or death. However, parapsychology studies show that precognitive information about future events is more likely to present itself to us in dreams than in any other fashion.

Many people who pay attention to their dreams discover that they have "little" precognitive dreams often. These concern upcoming events, situations and encounters with people. Such dreams seem to have the purpose of helping the dreamer prepare for the circumstances by previewing them.

Research at the Maimonides Medical Center in Brooklyn, New York, in the 1960s and 1970s demonstrated that information can be transmitted telepathically during dreaming, from a person who is awake to a person who is asleep. Of course, all this was known to ancient peoples!

Can people have the same dream at the same time?

Mutual dreaming, in which two or more persons share the same dream or same dream elements, is more common than one might think. We seldom discover this because, again, we don't pay attention to dreams and discuss them with others. Mutual dreaming is more likely to occur between or among people who have a close bond, either genetic or emotional, but can happen between persons who do not have a strong connection to one another. Mutual dreaming has not been explored much in research. It may have something to tell us about the interconnections of human consciousness.

Do sensory stimuli affect dreams?

Sounds, smells, tactile sensations and bodily functions can work their way into dreams and become part of the dream drama. For example, if you lose your bedcovers during the night, you may dream of being in a snow-covered place and feeling cold. A car alarm going off down the street may become a fire engine in a dream. Falling out of bed can appear in a dream in which you are falling from a great height. Having to urinate during the night can become a dream in which you are urinating. Being thirsty can manifest in a dream as you drinking water. Sigmund Freud found that by eating anchovies or highly salted foods prior to sleep, he caused himself to dream that he was drinking water.

One of the most famous and dramatic examples of how sensory stimuli become woven into dreams was recorded in the nineteenth century by Alfred Maury, a French scientist who studied dreams. One night he dreamed that he was

taking part in murders during the reign of terror in the
French Revolution. He was summoned before the tribunal,
where he saw Robespierre, Marat and other famous persons. He was tried and sentenced to death by guillotine. A
great crowd watched as he was led to a scaffold and tied to
the guillotine. He felt the blade sever his head and awoke
in terror. He discovered that a rail of his headboard had
come loose and fallen on the back of his neck—just like a
guillotine.

Sensory stimuli should be taken into account, but the
dream should not be dismissed. The dreaming consciousness makes use of whatever raw material it has to present
information. Dreamwork should be done on these dreams,
too.

Is it safe to work with dreams?

Dreams deal with our true—and often unexpressed or
unacknowledged—emotions, and with material in the subconscious. Anytime we examine what is below the surface,
unsettling emotions can result. Sometimes it may be advisable to do dreamwork with a therapist. In earlier days of
psychotherapy, it was considered unwise for people to examine their dreams without a therapist. Today, however, lay
dreamwork has proved fruitful and beneficial. The prevail-
ing wisdom about dreams is that they are inherently healing
in nature, and that they do not bring forth anything we are
not ready to examine.

What does sleepwalking have to do with dreams?

Most ordinary sleepwalkers are not acting out dreams.
In some cases, especially among children, sleepwalking fol-

lows night terrors, in which sleepers have a sensation of being choked or having a heavy weight on the chest.

Some sleepwalking and other actions during sleep are part of a condition called REM sleep behavior disorder, or RBD or RSBD. Many of these cases involve violent or destructive behavior that accompanies REM dreams that are excessively vivid and active. Sufferers of RBD, most of whom are men, have been known to jump from windows, get up and knock into furniture, drive cars, climb ladders and even attack their sleeping mates—all while they are asleep and having vivid dreams.

Isolated cases of acting out dreams can be related to intense anxiety. One such case in my files is that of a thirteen-year-old girl. One night she was returning home with her mother in their car. As they pulled into their driveway, the car behind them followed. A man got out and approached the mother. He was lost and wanted to ask directions. Once the mother and daughter were inside the house, the mother admitted to the girl that she had been very frightened by the man, and was glad he had good intentions.

The episode caused a fear of vulnerability in the girl. She was reluctant to go to sleep at night, afraid that someone could break into the house and attack her while she slept. She left her bedroom door ajar so that she could better hear any noises. After several restless nights, she secreted a small kitchen knife under her pillow as protection. That night, she had a vivid dream in which she awakened to see a male assailant coming through her bedroom door. Screaming, she leaped up out of bed with the knife and started swinging it at him. She awakened to find herself screaming and stabbing at her mother. The mother had got-

ten up in the middle of the night to go to the bathroom
across the hall from the daughter's bedroom. Seeing the
girl's door ajar, she pushed it open to check on her, when
the girl jumped up screaming and wielding the knife. Fortunately, no one was hurt.

Once the vulnerability issue was resolved, the girl had
no further episodes of acting out during dreaming, or of
nightmares of being attacked in her bedroom.

Can I control my dreams?

Dreams seem to have a mind of their own, but with good
purpose—they present to us what needs our attention.
Learning how to dream lucidly is one way to control dreams.
Another, more common way—and one used by peoples
around the world since ancient times—is to direct dreams
through incubation, a process in which we ask dreams to
answer a specific question. We've all had experiences in
which the answer to a problem or dilemma has become
clearer once we've "slept on it." With the conscious mind
out of the way, the intuition has a chance to communicate
through dreams.

Incubation techniques have been complicated rituals in
times past. But the same results can be obtained with simple
procedures. First, frame a clear question. Write it down,
repeat it to yourself and think about it during the day. Be
willing to accept what your intuition gives you as the answer.
Eat a light evening meal (some people prefer to fast) and
avoid stimulants and depressants. Thus, you will be less
likely to experience interrupted sleep throughout the night.
Prior to sleep, spend some quiet time in meditation thinking
about your question. Repeat the question to yourself as you

fall asleep, along with the assertion that you will dream the answer.

When you awaken, immediately record whatever you can remember, even if only fragments. When you have the opportunity, work with the dream—the answer may not be readily apparent.

Sometimes the answer will be clear upon awakening, even though you may not recall a dream. Other times, you may have to repeat the incubation process.

TWO

A Dreamwork Action Plan

How to Work with Dreams

Many techniques exist for working with dreams. Dreamwork is highly subjective, and I advise people to try different approaches and use what works best for them. I'll share with you the techniques that have worked the best for me, and which I use in working with groups.

A dream seldom has just one message. Because symbols are intuited rather than defined, they can be read in different ways, and each way can have meaning for the dreamer. A dream is likely to have a primary message, but also to have one or more secondary messages as well. The messages may all relate to the same situation, or may address multiple things going on in your life.

Our dreams are highly emotional, and give us feedback on how we are dealing with life situations emotionally. Dreams especially reveal our fears and anxieties, which is why so many of them seem negative. Working with dreams gives us insight into how we can deal with stresses, limiting belief patterns, obstacles, stressful situations and so on. Dreaming, even about negative situations and feelings, is positive and beneficial, because we are given insight into how to restore balance in life. Doesn't everyone want to know how to be happier and more fulfilled? Dreamwork helps us find the answers and the ways.

There is only one "rule" in dreamwork: only the dreamer can truly interpret his or her own dreams. When dreamwork is done in a group, others project their own meanings in a commentary as if the dream were theirs. Many projections resonate with a dreamer and stimulate fresh insights. Dream dictionaries and dreamwork books also provide ideas and insights. The dreamer must take the input and apply it to his or her own situation. The meaning of a dream will always be filtered through your own experience, knowledge and beliefs.

If you're curious about your dreams, make a commitment now to spend some time with them. Simply setting your intention to understand this part of yourself will invite your dream life to become more active. Be willing to work regularly with dreams. You can't really learn a language if you practice it only once a month. If you are able, work with dreams every day, or at least once or twice a week. Some dreams are more understandable than others, but even the most obscure fragments can contain pearls.

Dreams are very easy to forget, which is why it is especially important that you record a dream as soon as possible upon awakening. If you can't write it down, tape record it, tell it to someone else, or even tell yourself. Then write the dream down when you have the opportunity.

Written dreams become your historical record. It will be much easier to do dreamwork from a written account. Over time, you will notice patterns and the repetition of certain themes and symbols, which will give you additional insights.

Improving Intuition

Dreamwork improves intuition, and exercises to improve your intuition will benefit your dreamwork. Allowing your intuition to have a stronger voice will enable you to make better decisions. My book *Breakthrough Intuition* offers a program of ninety-four intuition-building exercises that you can easily incorporate into daily life, and which will in turn benefit your dreamwork.

Improving Your Recall

Everyone has trouble from time to time remembering dreams. This is natural—we go through phases when dream messages may be less pressing. Sometimes external stresses, travel, dietary changes, medications and health challenges can disrupt dream recall as well.

Paying attention to dreams stimulates improved recall for many people. Another helpful technique is programming yourself with affirmations, especially at bedtime, to remember your dreams: "I will remember my dreams" or "I will remember my dreams in as much detail as possible." Try a gentle herbal sleep tea, which may help you sleep without interruption.

Some people simply have a more difficult time than others remembering dreams. They may think that this means they are not getting the guidance and information that others receive from dreams. I believe that our intuition always reaches us, through synchronicity, inspiration and other ways, as well as through dreams. Dreaming is processing, and the results of the processing are accessible to us. Sometimes when I have done dream incubations to ask for dreams to answer a specific question, I do not remember a dream, but the answer is clear to me when I awake.

If you have difficulty remembering dreams, invite your intuition to present you with what you need to know. Pay attention to signs and insights, and especially body clues. Intuition often signals us through physical signs, such as a tightness or expansive feeling in the gut, chills and tingles in the skin.

Symbols and Plays on Words

Dreams use symbols and plays on words to get across a message. Symbols and plays on words are compact ways of delivering a lot of information. Symbols embody more than words; they are understood on an intuitive level as well as on a rational level. Plays on words involve homonyms and synonyms, puns, slang and idioms.

Consider the following dream:

I am going to work. I am just about to enter the building when I look down into the grassy area by the front door and see a huge snake coiled up, hiding in the grass. Somehow I know it intends to bite me. I stand paralyzed while other people go past me into the building, as though they don't know what's happening, or they don't care. The dream ends before anything happens.

The dreamer, a young man, worked in a competitive business, and had recently taken a new job in a company where he was regarded as up-and-coming talent. In real life, there was no grassy area in front of the building where he worked—it was all concrete, an urban environment where one would not find snakes. Asked if he could think of anyone who might be a "snake in the grass," that is, secretly lying in wait to do him harm, he had an immediate hit. He suspected that one of his new colleagues was secretly resentful and jealous of him, though this person often went out of his way to be nice and helpful. "I haven't been able to put my finger on anything," the dreamer said. "And I've been feeling bad about being suspicious when he's done so much to make me feel part of the team."

The dream confirmed his intuitive feelings, however, and gave him a warning to be careful of this person. A situation later developed at work that bore out the validity of the dream warning.

Here's another example of how dreams use plays on words:

I'm riding in a small airplane in the cockpit. We're flying along and then suddenly the plane goes into a nosedive. Nothing stops it and we crash into the ground. Strangely, I'm not hurt—I just seem to walk away. But the plane is demolished.

Airplanes can symbolize riding too high (not being grounded) or "flying high" (being successful or in good spirits) or being able to rise up and see the big picture. The dreamer was not a pilot. Here the key phrase is "goes into a nosedive." The dreamer was involved in a high-risk financial deal that seemed to be "flying along." The dreamer acknowledged that it was the sort of deal that could suddenly turn sour with very little warning—that is, go into a nosedive. The dream reflected his underlying anxiety that the whole thing would crash, for if it did, he would lose his money and thus his ability to make another investment (the demolished airplane). The dreamer had been telling himself not to worry—but his dream revealed how he honestly felt. What's more, the dream repeated, a sign of a pressing concern that needs to be addressed. The dreamer decided to sell his share of the deal and seek another, less risky one within his comfort zone.

Patterns and Personal Signatures

As your dreamwork builds, you will notice certain patterns in your dreaming. These may be clustered around temporary situations, or may occur throughout life. Dreamwork will also reveal to you your own personal dream "signatures." Everyone has a personal dream dictionary. When personal signatures show up in dreams, you know what they mean specifically to you. Personal signatures can be emotional tones, physical sensations or certain imagery. For example, Brenda Mallon, an inspirational therapist and author of *Dreams, Counselling and Healing* and other books, dreams of bears whenever major changes are about to occur in her life. Bears are strong, fierce and protective. The bear dreams initiate an internal gearing up for change. Mallon's conscious recognition of this personal signature gives her an advantage in meeting change.

One of my own personal signatures is the black-and-white dream. I usually dream in color, as do most people. Whenever I have a dream in black and white, I know that this is a signal to pay extra attention.

Seven Keys for Dreamwork

Here are seven keys for dreamwork that I have found to be highly effective:

1. ***Determine the high concept.*** The high concept of a dream is the distilled essence or theme of the dream, and will help you find the important thread or theme. One of the best ways to express the high concept is to give the dream a title.

2. ***Dissect the dream.*** Examine the elements of the dream, such as your emotions within the dream and upon awakening; dominant colors, sounds, textures, smells; other people present in the dream; setting and action in the dream, and so on. Which elements command your attention the most?

Use free association with the different elements. In free association, allow yourself to make spontaneous connections. For example, the house in the dream reminds you of _____, which in turn reminds you of _____ and makes you think of _____. Free association helps you to make inspired insights that might be missed under an analytical approach. Be uninhibited—don't worry how silly some associations may sound.

3. *Make personal associations.* One way of looking at a dream is to consider that all the elements in it—including other people, animals, landscapes and inanimate objects—represent something within you. Look at the various elements and determine what they say about you. Consider attitudes, beliefs, fears, behavior patterns, desires, wishes, goals and so on.

Pay special attention to emotions, both in the dream and upon awakening. Sometimes the scenarios of dreams really are about our emotions and our emotional responses to situations. For example, a middle-aged man long out of school periodically dreams of being back in high school, where he has to take a test for which he is unprepared. This is a common dream theme and often reflects anxieties about being adequately prepared in some other way. Another way of looking at the dream is to relate the emotions in the dream to the same emotions present in a current situation. The dreamer also could think back to that time in high school and relate emotions or situations then to present emotions and situations. Perhaps the dream might be saying, "Every time I am about to be tested in some way, I get unnecessarily panicky. I need to relax and be more confident."

4. *Make archetypal associations.* Some dreams seem especially important, powerful and charged with energy. Jung called these "big" dreams. Many big dreams come when we are grappling with important decisions or going through major life changes. Big dreams also occur when we go inward in the study of philosophy, spirituality and psychology, and when we face significant health challenges. Sometimes big dreams occur as markers along the path of life.

Any dream can have archetypal symbols; big dreams especially contain them. Archetypal symbols impress us as larger than life, perhaps even having a cosmic import. For example, a river in a dream can relate to where you are going in terms of a particular situation, and on an archetypal level address your "River of Life" direction.

I always recommend keeping a good dictionary of dream or mythological symbols handy for archetypal insights. Remember that such a dictionary will not define your dream for you, but will provide possible meanings and associations. Use what your intuition tells you fits your dream. Try my *Encyclopedia of Dreams: Symbols and Interpretations*, which features common dream symbols. The following chapters in this book present numerous examples of how common symbols and themes are portrayed in dreams, with both personal and archetypal associations. Use them for ideas and inspirations about your own dreams.

5. *Look for the spiritual dimension or "big picture."* Dreams tell us about our sense of our purpose in life, our worldview, our spiritual (and not necessarily religious) beliefs, and our sense of connection to something greater than ourselves. Some dreams are more obviously

spiritual than others. Always look for secondary spiritual messages and threads. Dreamwork shows us how to look at the parts of dreams, but the dream itself is holistic. My book *Dreamwork for the Soul* delves into the spiritual, transpersonal, mystical and paranormal aspects of dreams, which are an important part of our life alchemy and our understanding of the meaning of life.

6. *Expand on the dream.* Here are different techniques for getting more insights:

▪ Conduct a dialogue with the various elements of your dream, whether a person or an object. Ask the person or thing what its message is for you. This type of dialogue is called gestalt, and was pioneered by the Freudian-trained analyst Fritz Perls.

▪ Describe everything in the dream as though you were explaining it to someone who knows nothing about you. Use a real friend, an imaginary friend, or write it down or tape record it.

▪ Review your written account of the dream and pay special attention to the verbs. Are they similar? Do they repeat? For example, are you repeatedly running or shouting? Next, look at the adjectives you used in describing the dream. Verbs and adjectives are energy words and can put the dream content into perspective.

▪ Use active imagination. Reenter the dream and allow it to finish as a sort of daydream. Or, you can take a more assertive role by changing the dream action and outcome. Do dreamwork on what happens in the exercise.

- Meditate on a dream or symbols within a dream. Meditation stimulates the intuition to provide new insights. Jung often meditated upon his puzzling dreams. Sometimes he put in a lot of thought and effort, but he said the results were always worthwhile.

- Draw or paint your dream. Drawing and painting dreams often reveals what has not been, or cannot be, expressed by words. Keep a box of crayons and a tablet of drawing paper handy in case you feel inspired to sketch.

- Other creative ways to explore your dream include dancing it, and working in mixed media to create dream masks, tools, fiber art, and so on.

7. *Take action.* The process of dreaming is incomplete without action. Dreams provide information and insight for positive change in life. Without action, we do not gain. Recurring dreams often address especially pressing needs to change. Over and over again, the dreams ask us to pay attention, to act.

Action does not have to mean major change, although sometimes that's the case. Action can be as simple as acknowledging the message of the dream.

Dreamwork Ethics

It's fun and very productive to work with others on dreams. I have received some of my best insights into dreams in group settings. If you wish to work with others, keep these ethics in mind:

• Remember that only the dreamer can interpret the dream. Your projections, or commentaries, as they are called in group dreamwork, can be important to help the dreamer better understand the dream. There is no right or wrong. Respect the dreamer's own evaluation. Never tell a dreamer, "This is what your dream means." When offering your projection, couch it in first-person language: "If this were my dream, I would . . ." Leave the dreamer free to assimilate what fits.

• Be mindful of personal integrity, dignity and privacy. Dreamworking with others is most productive when everyone feels free to reveal personal matters. Everyone in the group should be aware that dreamwork sometimes brings unexpected and intense emotions and issues to the surface. Sometimes a dreamer chooses to keep something private or discontinue working on a dream in a group setting. Respect personal space. Dreamwork should remain confidential and never leave the group. Another's dream and personal life are not fodder for casual social conversation. If you wish to use someone's dream as an example, obtain permission.

• Dreamwork outside a clinical setting is not a substitute for psychotherapy or other professional treatment.

Further information about dreamwork ethics is available from the Association for the Study of Dreams. See the appendix for contact information.

Common dream symbols and themes are explored in the remaining chapters. Most of the examples are taken from my own collection of the dreams of others, used with permission. I have given the dreamer's interpretations and in some cases my own projections. Where possible, I have noted action taken by the dreamer. Some of the dreams come from published sources, and those are noted with citations in the endnotes. The examples feature some of the many ways symbols can be portrayed in dreams. They are not to be taken as definitive to all dreams containing the same symbols.

You will find many resonances with dreams of your own. Keep in mind that each chapter examines pieces of dreams. All the pieces of a dream fit together into a whole, which will have meaning within the context of your life and the spectrum of your experiences, beliefs, emotions and desires.

THREE

Flying and Falling

Dreams of flying and falling are the two most common themes reported in dreams throughout history. Flying dreams tend to be happy ones, while falling dreams are often nightmares. Both may be vivid and realistic, as though they are actually happening to the dreamer. Dream researchers have related flying and falling dreams to somatic sensations. Rhythmic breathing, pressures on the chest during sleep, and an activation of the central nervous system during REM periods are associated with flying dreams. Sleep paralysis is associated with falling dreams. The paralysis, a total relaxation of major muscles, is a natural condition during REM sleep. Some people may not dream of falling, but of running in slow motion or being unable to move in the presence of some danger.

While physiological factors may indeed play a role in flying and falling dreams, I agree with dream researchers who also see the symbolic importance of such dream content.

Flying

The sensation of flying is one of the earliest to appear in dreams during childhood. It becomes less and less frequent as we age; it especially diminishes with the onset of middle age. Flying dreams in which we rise into the air under our own power are almost always pleasant, even ecstatic and exhilarating. Here are examples of typical dreams about flying, floating and weightlessness:

I have a recurring dream in which I decide I want to fly. I run along the ground, sort of like a plane taking off, and rise up into the air. I fly around and do loops, feeling very happy. I'm sad when I wake up and the dream ends.

Suddenly I'm weightless and I levitate into the air. This happens every now and then in my dreams, and sometimes I can control my movements. Sometimes as soon as I realize I can control myself, the dream ends.

I "wake up" in the dream and find myself flying around my room just under the ceiling. I'm always filled with this incredible joy. If a long time goes by and I don't have a flying dream, I miss them.

I have the ability to go wherever I wish. As soon as I think about a place, I am there. It seems that I am weightless and fly or transport myself instantaneously.

I float downstairs in my house instead of walk down the stairs.

*I'm dancing, doing graceful whirls and pirouettes, just like a pro-
fessional ballerina. My movements become more and more in slow
motion, like time is stretched. I have a partner, and he lifts me up
like a ballerina. I become more and more weightless, until he lifts
me up and I rise into the air on my own.*

*I'm jumping up and down. Every time I jump, I go higher and
higher, and I feel more and more weightless. It takes longer for me
to float to the ground.*

Flying dreams like these have been recorded around the
world since ancient times. Everyone has a flying dream at
some point; many people have them frequently. The desire
to fly, to transcend the limits of the physical world, is deeply
embedded in human consciousness. Not only is flying
among the first dreams we have in life, it is one of the final
sensations of life as well. A weightless rising is sometimes
reported in the last moments of dying by those who are
lucid. Persons who have nearly drowned also report a pleasant sensation of rising upward just as they think they are
about to die.

We also associate flying with the spiritual. Divine and
semi-divine beings have the capability of flight. Enlightened
souls are lifted to heaven, and after death we can rise up to
heaven. Mystics, adepts, saints and the religious experience
ecstatic levitation and miraculous transport—the ability to
suddenly be at a distant location—as a result of their intense
spiritual practice and devotion.

What do flying dreams really mean? For most dreamers,
they are simply pleasurable experiences that seem to have

no particular meaning or purpose. Flying dreams may have various purposes, however, some related to states of consciousness and some to symbolic meaning in dreams.

In childhood, flying dreams may be related to fears and a need to escape them:

My first recollections of flying dreams go back to when I was a very little child, when we were living in London. The flying dream, when it first came, was connected with the sensation of fear. Halfway up the dimly lighted staircase that led to our nursery a landing opened on to a conservatory. The conservatory by day was a sunny place full of the pleasantest associations, but with the coming of darkness its character changed altogether. In the nighttime anything might be imagined to lurk in its unlighted corners; decidedly it was safest always to hurry past that landing, and even past other landings which, though they did not open on to any such dark spots, were not places where a child cared to linger alone. In some of the first dreams that I can remember I was on that staircase, fearful of something which I was especially anxious never to have to see. It was then that the blessed discovery was made, and that I found it was just as easy to fly downstairs as to walk; that directly my feet left the ground the fear ceased—I was quite safe; and this discovery has altered the nature of my dreams ever since. At first I only flew down one particular flight of steps, and always downwards; but very soon I began to fly more actively. If anything began to alarm me in my dreams, I used to rise in the air, but for some years I was unable to rise to any great height, or to fly with real ease. It was only gradually that the flying dream ceased to be connected with the sensation of fear and escape. For a long time it was often an effort to fly; every year, however, made it easier and more sure. By degrees "bad dreams" left me. When once I realized that I could always escape by flight, the sense of the something unknown, to be es-

caped from, became a thing of the past; but the power of flying grew and has steadily improved all my life.[1]

On a more esoteric note, flying dreams have been long associated with the ability of the soul to leave the body. Consider this dream recorded in the nineteenth century by Hervey de Saint-Denis, a French dream researcher:

Last night I dreamed that my soul had left my body, and that I was traveling through vast spaces with the rapidity of thought. First I was transported into the midst of a savage tribe. I witnessed a ferocious fight, without being in any danger, for I was invisible and invulnerable. From time to time, I looked towards myself, or rather towards the place where my body would have been if I had had one, and was able to reassure myself that I did not have one. The idea came to me to visit the moon, and immediately I found myself there. I saw a volcanic terrain with extinct craters and other details, obviously reproduced from books and engravings I had read or seen, but singularly amplified and made more vivid by my imagination. I was well aware that I was dreaming, but I was by no means convinced that the dream was entirely false. The remarkable clarity of everything that I saw gave rise to the thought that perhaps my soul had temporarily left its terrestrial prison, an occurrence that would be no more remarkable than so many other mysteries of creation. I remembered some of the opinions of the ancient authors on the subject, and then this passage from Cicero:

". . . If someone had risen into the heavens and had seen close up the sun, the moon and the stars, he would draw no pleasure from the experience unless he had someone to tell it to . . ."

Immediately I wished to return to earth; I found myself back in my bedroom. For a moment I had the strange sensation of looking at my sleeping body, before taking possession of it again. Soon I thought that I had got up and with pen in hand was noting down in detail everything that I had seen. Finally I awoke, and a thousand details which had recently been so clear in my mind faded almost instantly from my memory.[2]

Saint-Denis's experience of losing the details at the very point of awakening is a common one. We often dream in such vividness that we think we can never forget even the minutest detail—yet everything evaporates when we reenter waking consciousness.

His dream was lucid—he knew that he was dreaming while he was dreaming. Flying is a common characteristic of lucid dreaming; likewise, many flying dreams are lucid ones. If we accept the premise that the dreaming consciousness extends beyond the body, then flying dreams offer us a distinct awareness of being apart from the body, more so than "ordinary" dreams.

The purpose of flying dreams may be the sheer joy and exhilaration they bring—perhaps these intense emotions are necessary to our overall health and well-being. They may also serve an important function of expanding our awareness of the reach of consciousness, that we are truly multidimensional beings. They may also enhance our own powers of creativity. It is significant that flying dreams start early in life and are prominent in childhood, when imagination and possibility are unfettered. The child's horizon is unlimited. Limits are created by conditioning and disappointing experiences. By middle age, our horizons may have shrunk a great deal. We think less of what is still possible than what is no longer possible, or what we did not do when we had the chance.

Sometimes flying dreams seem more tied to dream symbolism. Like airplane dreams, they may be telling us of a childish desire to escape circumstances rather than face them, or that we may not be grounded, or that we are indulging in fantasy. Consider the following dream:

> *I'm being pursued by a mob of angry people. I escape them by lifting up into the air on my own and flying away.*

For this dreamer, flight clearly meant escape from unpleasant circumstances. He was heavily in debt through bad spending habits and easy credit. The angry mob represented the institutions and people to whom he owed money. Collections agencies were calling him, and friends no longer opened their wallets. Rather than face his situation and look for a constructive solution—such as a plan for repayment— he wished to run away from it all.

This dream was a repeating one. Dreamwork helped the young man to be realistic about his situation. He was not going to magically escape. Facing the consequences of his irresponsibility would not be pleasant, but he had to do it.

Many dreamers discover that they can will themselves to have flying dreams through autosuggestion:

> *I found that if I steadily thought about such a dream as the flying dream it would soon come back. It will not, indeed, come exactly to order, but it will come after a short interval. I have never been able exactly to measure this interval; it may be two or three nights, or it may be longer, varying very much according to the definiteness with which the waking mind has concentrated upon the idea. Especially after talking about flying I find that I am certain very soon to dream about it.[3]*

The power of suggestion also works if a dreamer begins to lose the power of flight in a dream, and floats or falls down:

At such moments the "word of power" comes into my mind, and I repeat to myself, "You know that the law of gravitation has no power over you here. If the law is suspended, you can fly at will. Have confidence in yourself, and you need not fear." Confidence is the one essential for successful flight, and confidence thus being restored, I find that I can fly again with ease.[4]

There is a deeper message in flying dreams that applies to us all. If the law of gravitation is a symbol for limitation (especially self-imposed), then flying dreams teach us to reach for our highest potential, the dream of reality that seems out in the stars. We know from the history of art, invention, innovation and genius that human beings are capable of magnificent greatness. Dreams are a gentle way of preparation. They provide a safe way to soar. But it is up to us to heed our dreams, take confidence in our abilities, and turn them into reality.

Falling

Like flying dreams, falling dreams are more common in childhood than later in life. Sometimes they are related to feelings of vulnerability. Children, of course, feel vulnerable as they experience more of the world around them. As adults we feel vulnerable, too, when circumstances change and we go into a "freefall." Falling dreams occur during times of transition, when we are uncertain of ourselves and what is going to happen next. We fear a loss of something: status, money, self-esteem, material things, relationships. Dream studies show that more men than women report falling dreams. Falling dreams also are part of flying dreams— first we fly, then we fall.

In falling dreams, we may fall ourselves, watch ourselves fall, watch somebody else (who symbolizes us) fall, or have a fear of falling. We may watch somebody else (representing a part of us) start to fall, and then become that person as we fall.

Falling dreams are characterized by intense emotions: panic, fear, confusion, uncertainty, dread. Sometimes there is a calm resignation to the fate of falling.

I'm standing in front of a tall office building, looking up. I see a figure lean out of a window and plummet toward the ground. Suddenly I'm the one who's falling. I think, "This is just the way it has to be." I wake up before I hit.

This dream occurred to a man whose company had been acquired in a hostile takeover, and his job future was uncertain. He was worried about how he would meet his financial obligations, and also resigned to whatever might happen—his fate was beyond his control. He also saw meaning in the phrase "falling down on the job." He felt under enormous pressure to perform well under the new regime.

The following repeating dream was more vague, and puzzled the dreamer.

I've had this dream for years. All of a sudden I'm aware that I'm falling through black space. There's no top, no bottom. I wake up in a panic.

The dreamer had low self-esteem. In almost any social situation, she imagined that others were sizing her up and thinking negative things about her. She literally was in a free fall of anxiety.

Many people have heard that if you fall in a dream and hit bottom before you wake up, it means you die in your sleep, or you are going to die. This is an unfounded superstition. The panic of falling will often wake a dreamer up, but it is not unusual to dream of striking a surface.

I dreamed I was being forced by a threatening, savage-looking man to jump off a cliff. I hit a bunch of rocks below. It hurt like hell.

The dreamer was undergoing a painful and "savage" transition in life. It hurt, but from the dream he knew he would be all right in the outcome.

I fell from some height and sort of floated to the bottom. I landed on my feet and walked away.

This dream told the dreamer that the changes he was going through were not as devastating as he feared.

Falling into pits and holes can symbolize a "pit of despair" or "being in the hole" financially or as an outcast.

Falling dreams, especially if they repeat, may be signals to the dreamer to take more control, shore up self-esteem, and look for ways to rise up over obstacles.

FOUR

The Body and Bodily Functions

Did you ever think your feet might have a message for you in your dreams? Or your hands? They do—as do other parts of the body, and bodily functions. Whenever your attention is called to your body, look for a symbolic meaning.

Teeth

We dream about our teeth more than any other body part. One of the most common dreams is that of teeth becoming loose and/or falling out. It's a motif that puzzles many people, especially when it repeats in dreams, such as this one:

I keep dreaming that I suddenly notice that several of my teeth 41
are real loose. I'm afraid to touch them because if I do, I'm convinced
they will fall out. It's terrifying.

DREAMSPEAK

The dreamer was in a job grown stale and no longer felt challenged. He would complain, "I don't have anything to do that I can sink my teeth into." Additionally, he felt powerless to change his situation. He had worked for many years for the same company, and was afraid that changing jobs would jeopardize his security. He felt secure, but bored, and increasingly unimportant.

The loose-teeth dream was repeating to call attention to the imbalance in his life. Teeth are symbols of personal power. The connection between the loose teeth and his complaint had an impact on the dreamer, and he realized he needed to take action. But after a long self-examination, he decided that he did not want to leave his employer. However, he did resolve to find ways to enhance his job, and to change his attitude about it. He shifted some attention to the various benefits the job provided: security, regular hours, ample vacation time, and so on. He policed his complaining, and whenever he caught himself doing so, he would replace the complaint with a positive statement. Over time, he restored his sense of being in control, and the loose teeth dreams ceased.

This loose-teeth dream addressed a relationship problem:

Two teeth fall out while I am chewing gum—one upper and one lower, both on the right side. I worry whether the gum chewing did it—I chewed even though I could feel them getting loose—and I worry whether more will fall out, and if I will still be attractive.

The dreamer had been involved in a relationship that was destructive, but she felt unable—or was unwilling—to get out of it. The boyfriend was a gum chewer, a habit the woman did not like but picked up. Her association with the gum chewing was that she was "gumming things up" by staying in the relationship, even though she knew it was not good for her. The upper tooth and lower tooth that fell out signified her power loss in her upper and lower worlds, emotional/spiritual and physical. Her concern about remaining attractive reflected her deeper concern for her own well-being. This dream was part of a larger syndrome of dreams giving her the same message about the relationship, and her dreamwork played a role in her successful termination of it.

The next dream deals with a dreamer's attempt to make accommodations:

My teeth hurt. They also seem to be misaligned in my jaw. I can push them around in my mouth. I try to rearrange them so they fit better. Then I see that they are all loose and about to fall out. I look at myself in the mirror. Several teeth fall out when I open my mouth. I think I'm going to lose all of them.

The dreamer's company had been acquired in a takeover, and he had been reassigned to a new division with a new boss. He was grateful not to be out of a job, as were many of his coworkers, but he did not like the new setup. He was trying to accommodate himself to the circumstances, telling himself this was for the best. His repeating dream was telling him otherwise, however. No matter how he tried to fit the new circumstances, he wasn't happy.

Most teeth dreams feature loss of teeth. The next dream

is different—it features new teeth coming in to replace the ones that are lost.

I'm looking in the mirror and feel my front teeth are loose. As I look, they actually fall out into my hands. Then I see that new teeth are coming in.

For the dreamer, a woman in a top-level job, her front teeth symbolized her "upfront" image and responsibilities. For some time, she had been losing interest in her job, however, and was putting increasing amounts of time into other pursuits that she found more interesting and fulfilling. The new teeth represented these other pursuits. She felt the dream was showing her that her heart was no longer in her job, but was in a new profile that she was creating for herself.

Both this and the preceding dream feature looking into a mirror. This image appears often in dreams, whether about teeth or something else. Mirrors are symbols of truth—they reflect things as they are, not as we wish them to be. Looking into a mirror in a dream often means confronting the truth about something.

Eyes

Our eyes are our greatest connection to others. It is said that the eye is the window of the soul. One's eyes reveal all emotions, as well as provide a gauge of character, honesty and truth.

A person who has animal eyes in a dream might be expressing the essence or truth of that animal, and its symbolic associations.

In this dream, an extra eye takes on significance:

> *I am looking into the mirror. I can't see myself clearly—my face goes in and out of focus. When it comes into focus, I see that I have a great big eye in the center of my forehead, in addition to my regular eyes.*

To the dreamer, the third eye literally symbolized "the third eye" of psychic ability and intuition. In esoteric science, the third eye is at a chakra point in the middle of the brow. The dreamer was in the middle of a series of classes on developing the intuition. The dream told her that a new way of seeing was coming into focus.

In the next dream, an eye is the source of a wounding:

> *I awaken from sleep and find that one eye (my right eye) is bleeding at the corner, as though I am weeping blood. When I wipe it away, I find that it is thick and gelatinous. I am so shocked and think that it can't be so, that I go through the awakening again in the dream, only to find my eye still seeping blood. I panic that this is a sign of one of those horrible diseases, like Ebola, where you bleed through your orifices before you die. I tell someone (a man), "I am bleeding through my orifices!" even though the eye is not an orifice.*

Weeping blood symbolizes a wound so deep that our very vital being is threatened. The dreamer did feel mortally in danger. The dream addressed a severely distressing personal situation, and her ability to "see right" about it. When she referred to the relationship, she said it was "killing her."

As will be seen about blood symbolism later in this chapter, the seeping away of blood often represents something that is draining us physically, emotionally and spiritually.

Hands

After our eyes, our hands are the most expressive part of the body, especially of emotions and actions. There is little thought, feeling or intent that cannot be expressed solely with the hands. In art and symbolism, hands say far more than words.

The hand is a symbol of strength, authority and power, a meaning dating to the ancient Egyptians, whose term for the hand also related to pillar and palm. Hands also symbolize our creativity and action in the material world—our deeds and accomplishments.

An eye associated with a hand—in a dream, this might be represented by a hand pointing to an eye—means clairvoyant vision, or a wise, all-seeing vision. The hand of God, or divine power or intervention, is often represented by a hand of light reaching down through clouds. The gods of antiquity healed by touch; thus the hand is considered to possess great healing and generative power.

The right hand is the hand of power that gives, transfers and confers, while the left hand is the hand of receptivity and submission. The left hand also is associated with dishonesty and cheating. In esoteric spiritual science, the right hand signifies the masculine principle and rational, conscious thought, and the left hand signifies the feminine principle and intuitive, unconscious thought. Clasped hands thus symbolize the mystic marriage of opposites that creates wholeness and completeness, and also the communication between the conscious and unconscious. Clasped hands also symbolize the unbreakable emotional bonds between persons, especially marriage and fidelity. This is why clasped hands are part of our popular wedding imagery.

Other meanings of hands that can be demonstrated in dreams are:

Shaking hands or offering a hand: friendship, devotion, forgiveness

Open hands or palms turned up: receptivity, especially in terms of prayer and divine blessings

Raised hands with palms up: worship; or, amazement

Raised hands with palms out: blessing, favor, healing

Raised hands above head or folded in front of body: submission, surrender

Raised hand(s) to mouth: silence, caution, warning

Raised hands to head: thought

Outstretched hands: welcoming, protection

Relaxed hands at sides: confidence

Outstretched hands with palms raised outward: warding off

Closed hands: unwillingness, secrets

Closed hands within folded arms: denial, being threatened

Clenched hands: aggression

Clean hands: purity

Dirty hands: dishonesty, unpleasantness

Tied hands: powerlessness

Empty hands: poverty, lack, loss

Full hands: abundance, bounty, success

Caressing hands: love, concern, tenderness

Laying on of hands: healing, transfer of power or authority, benediction

Clapping hands: approval

The dreamer who had the third eye dream had this dream about her hand:

I am with J. and she has a cat, a gray-and-yellow tabby (female). I go to pet the cat and it bites me on the right hand, the fourth and fifth fingers. The bite is so hard that I fear the bones will break. It is excruciatingly painful, and the cat hangs on and on. I finally get my hand free. I have deep puncture wounds that are not bleeding much. I tell J. about her cat biting me, and she seems unconcerned.

J. was a good friend of the dreamer's, but owned no cat. An animal bite can mean that the dreamer needs to absorb or take on some characteristic or quality related to the animal. The dreamer associated cats with intuition, mystery, independence and the feminine. In addition to her classes on developing the intuition, she also was taking instruction in energy healing. She felt the dream was telling her to trust her intuitive impressions more when she did energy healing with her hands. Her right hand was dominant. The cat hangs on to make sure she gets the message.

Feet

Feet can give us clues in dreams about how we are "walking our talk." Trudging along in heavy boots or shoes that hurt provide additional clues concerning how we are going about in life. Walking barefoot can refer to being well grounded or centered—having a sole or "soul" connection to the earth, or to life.

In this dream, barefoot takes on a different meaning:

I go to a meeting. When I get there, I discover that I have no shoes on—I'm barefoot.

This image could fit the "inappropriate dress" themes found in the next chapter on clothing and nudity that relate to being unprepared. But the dreamer recognized it as relating to sensitivity. Unless we go about barefoot quite a bit, our feet are tender and sensitive. The dreamer was sensitive about a controversial issue at work.

Heart

Dreams in which our hearts are prominent often concern emotional issues. They may also relate to something important—we use the expression "at the heart of the matter" to refer to the essential point. Hearts also symbolize valor and courage, as in the following dream:

I am starring as an actress in four one-act plays. They all have something to do with the heart, and each one has a lesson about the heart. Each heart for each play has a different color. As I wake up, it seems I can remember all four plays, but when I try to recall them, I can only remember two. One has a yellow heart (the first) and one has a purple heart.

In play #1 I am a medieval king or knight. It has something to do with hunting in the forest. I get killed by some sort of tragic accident. My role calls for me mostly to lie there playing dead while others talk. In play #2 I am a monk. That's all I remember.

Scene shifts: I have a notebook filled with pages and pages of handwritten material done in purple ink. I don't know about what.

I go to an amusement park that offers safe rides and watch others taking them. The equipment seems to be done in purple plastic. While I am there, I watch two flying boat rides. They are supposed to keep the cars from swinging close together, but someone lets them get too close. I know it's dangerous. There is also a very tame roller coaster.

Scene shifts: I am teaching a class about the hearts. I hand out stickers of glittery colored hearts for people to paste in their notebooks.

The dreamer recognized day residue in the dream—she had just finished reading a fantasy novel set in medieval times about fighting in the forest, and a king defending himself. He did not die in the novel.

The dominant themes in the collage of scenes relate to safety and playing it safe. In the first play, the dreamer has little challenge in the role of simply playing dead while others do the talking. She associated the yellow heart with lack of courage—perhaps the knight had died due to cowardice.

She associated the purple heart in the second play with

wisdom, regal bearing and valor. But her role as a monk meant she was shut away from the world—another kind of withdrawal.

At the amusement park, she watches others take rides. The rides are tame, but she doesn't even get on one herself. She is an observer, not a participant. There is only one ride that seems dangerous.

The dream expressed the passivity of the dreamer. She acknowledged that she often felt that life was passing her by while she watched. She did not like to take risks. The last scene underscores her detachment: the only thing she has to offer others are stickers of hearts.

The dream also showed a progressive passivity. At first she is a knight, a symbol of questing and the search to know one's self. But she gets killed, and after that her passivity increases: to the monk, and then to the observer, and then to the teacher who has nothing to say.

The dreamer could see this pattern in her own life. She felt she had this dream because deep inside she really didn't want to remain this way.

Missing or Damaged Body Parts

Missing, severed or injured body parts can deliver powerful symbolic messages about dysfunction in life and how we are being affected. This dream came to a woman who was in a relationship with an emotionally abusive partner. The imagery and impact were so shocking that the dreamer was moved to initiate therapy. Here is her description of the dream and the events that occurred afterward:

He [the partner] was dressed as a Nazi stormtrooper with a peaked cap and boots. He was holding my amputated legs in his hands. I was horrified and "woke up" to the nature of the relationship, that I was stymied and had lost my power to move.

I made an immediate appointment with a therapist. He was so threatened by this that he offered to go with me to the first appointment, but brought with him a yellow lined pad with a list of my faults that he read aloud to the therapist angrily. When she said, "You seem very angry," he stormed out of the room, slamming the door. She then asked me if this was the kind of relationship I wanted. When I finished crying she asked me to diagnose him, using my social-work skills (I was practicing at that time). I couldn't put on my thinking cap, I was too distraught. She then told me that he was very likely paranoid schizophrenic and not a candidate for therapy other than medication.

Thus began a long journey for me, a year's therapy into exploring why I had chosen such a partner and of course lots of working through of childhood relationships with narcissistic parents, whom he resembled in many ways. Major growth occurred. Sometimes it takes a crisis to move forward.

An abusive relationship does "cut the legs off" the victim, who often feels powerless to change things or to leave. In the dream, the partner has total control. By holding the dreamer's severed legs, he prevents her from going anywhere. His authoritative, abusive and cruel power is demonstrated by the Nazi stormtrooper image. Indeed, when given the chance to communicate in a neutral therapy forum, he "storms" around in anger.

In the following dream, the meaning of a missing limb is explained in a play on words:

I'm walking along a street when a threatening-looking man walks up, pulls a gun out of his coat and robs me. I am surprised to see he only has one arm. He has to reach out to grab my wallet with the same hand holding the gun. I know I could overpower him, but I don't—I let him take the wallet, which has a lot of money in it. There are lots of people around me, but nobody does anything.

The dreamer had a gambling compulsion and had lost a lot of his family's savings at the slot machines—also known as one-armed bandits. The dreamer felt guilty but also felt he had no control over his urge to gamble. He felt the dream was showing him he did have the ability to fight back and take control—nobody else could do it for him.

Waste Elimination

Dreams involving urination and defecation are common, and often seem to be the result of physical stimuli. For example, you have to urinate in the middle of the night, so you have a dream about it. But we must consider the whole story or we may be shortchanging ourselves out of an important message. There is symbolic meaning to elimination, too.

I do a great deal of urinating. I stand in line at a ladies' room. When I get to the toilet, I urinate an enormous quantity—I am surprised my bladder held so much. The stall is small and cramped and the toilet bowl very small. I squat over it and hope the stuff doesn't go all over. There is a man in attendance in the lavatory. I know him but I cannot recall his identity. The urination scene happens over again.

Urination often relates to creativity—something that flows forth from within. When we release creativity, sometimes we are surprised at how much we have within us. Such was the case with the dreamer of this dream, who was discovering her ability to paint and also needed to let her creativity expand.

Defecation also can relate to creativity—it is something solid that issues forth from the center of your being. It can also have a colloquial meaning: we use terms like *shit, poop* and *crap* to refer to something that's worthless. In this context, defecating into a toilet could symbolize something that has lost its value or needs to be flushed away.

Excrement, which is a fertilizer, also can symbolize the start of something new. This meaning is alchemical in nature. In alchemy, the old must putrefy (like waste) in order to create the new. Jung recognized that we must "dig through our own shit" in order to find gold (what is of true value) within.

In the next dream, excrement symbolizes an unpleasant situation:

I am walking through some sort of refugee camp. People are scattered around the ground on blankets. I am with two other women, and seem to be in a position of authority. We pass a young woman with long, black hair, with an infant. The infant is naked and I see it from the back side. It is defecating profusely, and the young woman keeps wiping it up with a small cloth. For reasons which are clear in the dream, but which I do not recall upon awakening, this shit-laden cloth must be disposed of immediately, and it falls to me to do it. I cannot hold it—it has to be out of sight. There are no garbage cans around, so I have no alternative but to place it in my mouth until I find a waste bin. It fills my mouth. I hold it lightly on the tongue, thinking I can stand it for a moment or two. But I can't find a garbage can anywhere. I walk and walk. When I finally find one, the shit-laden cloth has become a gummy, stinking ball. I spit it out. My mouth reeks of shit. I am disgusted.

The dreamer found the image of feces inside the mouth so overwhelmingly revolting that it was hard for her to find a positive message in the dream. In group dreamwork, the meaning quickly revealed itself. The dream reflected her true feelings about a job she was doing. She worked in public relations, and was promoting a message she was at odds with personally. She told herself she could divorce her personal feelings from her professional requirements. But her dream told her she was "full of shit" and "speaking shit." The excrement comes from the baby, an innocent source, who symbolized the client. The dreamer felt she had to "take care of the client's shit." Deep down inside, she was disgusted with herself for "selling out."

Working with this dream helped the dreamer to gain a better perspective on the situation—she admitted she had blown things out of proportion—and also helped her to know herself better.

Blood

Blood is a symbol of our emotions and our life force and vitality. When we're severely wounded emotionally, we often say we're bleeding, or our heart is bleeding. A loss of blood in dreams can represent something that is draining us emotionally, or even draining us physically, sapping our strength.

Blood also is a symbol of baptism, and so being awash in blood or bathed in blood can represent an initiation of a spiritual nature.

Blood flows can be cleansing, such as in a context where "old blood" or tainted blood is flowing out. Menstrual blood, a bodily function that cleanses the uterus, also has this connotation, as in this dream:

I'm in my room with a woman and we are talking. I am telling her about how sick I am of everyone else's mess. I see blood on my bed and say, "Who left that there?" Then I think maybe I got my period. I went to the closet and started cleaning by throwing things out the window. I wanted to call in sick so I could stay home and finish cleaning my house. I saved one object that was repairable— a vacuum cleaner.

Cleaning is the main theme in this dream. The dreamer does not want to clean up other people's messes, and feels an urgent need to clean her own house. The closet is emptied, apparently of broken items. The only thing salvageable is a cleaning tool—a vacuum cleaner. In waking life, the dreamer was discontented at work, feeling she indeed had to clean up messes made by others. The start of her period in the dream symbolized an internal cleaning of attitudes. The closet represents old stuff no longer needed. The word "sick" appears twice in the dream—a signal from the intuition that the dreamer's health was being affected by the stress and pressure she felt.

FIVE

Clothing and Nudity

We use clothing to make a statement to the world: we are conservative, hip, fashionable, wealthy, relaxed, confident, showy. Our clothing reflects how we want others to regard us. Clothes can make us appear to be something other than what we are. We use clothing to be inconspicuous, to hide shortcomings, flaws and faults. Or, we use it to draw attention to ourselves, to advertise our status or beauty.

Clothes in dreams are important symbols about our persona—the mask or face we present to the world. Each of us has a variety of masks that we wear every day—for example, in our career, as a parent, as a spouse, as a sibling, as a child, as a neighbor, as a spokesperson, an actor, and so on. According to Jung, problems arise if we have no developed persona for a situation, or if we allow one particular persona to take over our entire life. Anytime we make a significant change in job, relationships, school or home, our masks have to adjust to the new circumstances. Sometimes we have to let go of old ones and allow new ones to develop.

Changing Clothes

Dream clothing tells us how we feel about ourselves and how we think others see us. Shabby clothes, for example, tell us we don't feel good about ourselves, perhaps in general or concerning something we've done. Unhappy feelings about our clothing in dreams indicate the same. Changing clothing, or wanting to or trying to change clothing, indicates a change of direction, a new phase of life, or a reckoning with one's self—or the need to make such changes.

Women have more clothing dreams than men, and are more likely to notice clothing details in dreams. They also have more dreams about being inappropriately or inadequately dressed. This is not surprising, since women spend more time on their appearance than do men, worry about their appearance more than do men, and have more emotions invested in the impression they think they make on others.

Sometimes we don't see the significance of clothing in dreams. Being preoccupied with one's clothing can seem unimportant, as in the following dream:

I had a dream about my son who is now twenty-one years old. In the dream my son was around six or seven years old. I don't know whose house we were in. It was me, my husband and my son in the dream. My son started to have some sort of a seizure and we won-

dered if we should take him to the hospital (why we just didn't take him, I don't know). Well, we didn't take him and he returned to normal. But, the dream continued and he had another seizure. We decided to take him to the hospital, but I had to change my clothes, because the clothes I was wearing were just HORRIBLE (I just felt like I couldn't go anywhere in those clothes). Even though I knew we should hurry to get him help, I continued to look for clothes and couldn't find any. I would look in the closet (now this was my parents' house and my childhood bedroom and closet) and all the clothes were dirty and on the floor, there was nothing hanging up and clean. I looked and looked and couldn't find anything. After a while of looking, we were in the car taking him to the hospital and then my parents were with us in the car and my son was a baby and having another seizure and then that was the end of the dream. When I woke, I was wondering why I worried about changing my clothes. All day long, I worried if my son was OK.

Although the dreamer initially worried that the dream was about her son, it became apparent in dreamwork that the focus of the dream was her clothing—a symbol of her self-image. Her son represented herself in childhood. The dreamer was the only girl in a family of five children. Growing up in a farm community, she found that boys seemed to be valued more for their ability to work on the farm; she had to compete to prove her worth. Finding and building her sense of self-worth was an ongoing project throughout life. In the dream, she feels "horrible" about the clothing she is wearing, but can't find anything clean and suitable in her childhood closet. She feels unable to act—literally "go anywhere" in life—without the proper clothing. The dream was giving her several messages: how she felt about herself in childhood; her present discomfort with her "appearance," or the way she thought others viewed her; and the unsuitability of her old clothes, or self-image, for her present needs.

The age of her son in the dream was the approximate age at which she began to feel acutely inferior to her brothers. She was the fourth child and was six years old when her youngest brother was born. This brother was the apple of her parents' eye, and they always compared her to him. She felt she could never do anything right whenever he was involved.

The seizure could be seen as attempts to get attention for something that needed to be healed. She interpreted the passivity of her husband in the dream as meaning that changing her self-image was something only she could do for herself.

The dream obviously held a lot of power for the dreamer. It apparently was stimulated by her pursuit of spiritual study, which naturally would turn attention on self-image.

Several weeks later, the dreamer had other dreams that seemed to be related:

My son lost consciousness and we had to take him to the doctor, but in this dream I didn't have to change clothes, we left immediately.

The dreamer is not self-conscious about how she presents herself. Remedial action for healing is immediate; there is none of the wondering and second-guessing as in the previous dream. Another dream was this:

The dream started with my son missing. I was very distraught. My boss asked for my help at a big meeting, but the meeting wasn't work-related. There was a long conference table with people sitting around it that I didn't know. There were pretty dresses positioned around the table. My son had been missing for two weeks and I asked my boss for help finding him. He informed me that after two weeks he probably wouldn't be found. I started crying. Then the scene changed to a deserted street and I was having sex. Then the dream ended.

The dream indicates more inner shifting of a positive nature. The son, a symbol of the source that had a negative effect on her self-image, is now missing from the picture. The boss, an authority figure, is a symbol of the Higher Self—that part of us that knows what is best for us and sees the big picture. The dreamer's distress over the missing son represents an innate and common urge to hang on to old behavior patterns, even ones not in our best interests. The message from the boss/Higher Self, however, is to let go, which is distressing to the dreamer. It is hard to let go of what is familiar and known.

The clothing theme reappears here as the pretty dresses. They are choices for the dreamer. This is a personal issue, not work-related. The deserted street symbolizes the new territory to be filled in and mapped out for the new self-image. It doesn't have any landmarks yet.

Having sex in dreams often represents the desire to make something a part of ourselves. Here it shows that the dreamer is already leaving the old patterns behind and embracing a new one. "I feel like I have made spiritual progress," said the dreamer. "I feel myself becoming a more loving person."

Being inappropriately or inadequately dressed is a common dream, and can symbolize feelings of inadequacy, as in this example:

Some people come over for dinner. They seem to be friends or business associates of my husband's. I have cooked an elaborate dinner. But when the guests arrive, I somehow haven't changed into good clothes. I'm wearing some old, sacky thing. I'm embarrassed.

The dreamer had recently married a man whose job required a great deal of business entertaining. She had fears about what the people from "his world" would think of her—would they consider her an equal or see her for what she "really was"? The dream also contained a word play in the "old, sacky thing": it revealed her fears that she would be "sacked" or discarded after proving herself inadequate as a helpmate.

Dream clothing can tell us how we feel about new roles we have taken on in life. This dream followed the birth of a first child:

I'm going through my closet looking for something to wear. Nothing fits anymore, or looks right on me. I seem to have nothing but suits, and they are all out of style.

The dream reflected how the dreamer felt about her body—she was sensitive about the weight she gained during pregnancy, and desired to lose it. It was true that few of her pre-pregnancy clothes still fit her. But the dream also addressed her new self-image and her uncertainty about how her life would change. The dreamer had taken a leave of absence from her job, but was conflicted about going back into the workplace. She was uncertain that her career-oriented persona still fit in her new world as mother.

Anytime we make a change in life—such as moving to a new home, changing jobs or circumstances at work, taking on new responsibilities and tasks, entering new relationships and changing the dynamics of existing relationships—our persona or mask needs refitting. This process often is reflected in our dream clothing.

I have to get dressed for a special occasion—a banquet or something. I'm in a department store going through racks of clothes. A strange woman comes up to me. She is dressed in very old, even antique clothes. She looks very out of place. She holds out an outfit for me. It looks like an old style. I don't want to take it, but I don't want to offend her, either.

The dreamer was letting go of the old—things which no longer served her. Banquets are held to celebrate and honor. She was getting dressed—or molding a new persona—to fit her new self. The strange woman in the dream was her old self, that part of her that did not want to release old thought and behavior patterns, symbolized by the old and outdated clothing.

The imagery made the dreamer aware that she needed to push forward and not look back. "The old outfit that she was trying to give me looked comfortable," the dreamer said, "but I knew I didn't want to wear it." Old behavior patterns do indeed become comfortable. If we think we will not succeed, we build a comfort zone around us of not ever having to take risks and challenges. If we never try, we will never fail, so the reasoning goes. We succeed by default. The dreamer realized that it would be easy to fall back into old habits. She also realized that she needed to honor her old self for all the lessons learned.

The dreamer expanded on this dream in a waking dream meditation in which she reentered the dream and engaged the strange woman in conversation. She explained to the woman that she appreciated her interest, but the outfit was not her style, and she would choose one herself. She then went through the racks of clothing until her attention was captured by an outfit. It was a beautiful blue dress that fit perfectly and had a shimmer to it. It was definitely more showy than clothing she was accustomed to wearing. She put it on and turned to the woman and said, "Don't you think I look much better now?" The woman agreed.

This exercise carried a great deal of emotional satisfaction for the dreamer, who felt that she was truly stepping into a new self-image.

Sometimes inappropriate dream clothing speaks not to our fears about inadequacy, but to our real unsuitability in a role. Wallace B. Clift, a religious studies teacher and dream researcher, experienced inappropriate clothing in repeating dreams during a time he was considering changing careers:

Wallace, during the time he was a parish priest, used to dream that he arrived at the church without appropriate liturgical dress—a stole, for example. Though he liked the work of the parish priest, he would now understand such dreams as indicating that his truer call-

ing lay elsewhere. In teaching he has made a more comfortable ad-
aptation between the demands of the outer world and the movement
of his own individuation.[1]

Nudity

One of the most common dreams is to have no clothing on at all. Such dreams often cause great embarrassment, both in the dream and after awakening, especially if they repeat. Here are examples of nudity dreams:

> *I'm walking down a street and I go into a shop to buy something. I suddenly discover that I am completely naked. I'm horribly embarrassed and try to cover myself. The odd thing is, nobody else seems to notice that I'm not wearing any clothes.*

> *I'm at a party with G. Not only am I nude, but I am the only person there who has no clothes on. I feel very exposed and wonder if people are staring at me.*

In the first example, the dreamer acknowledged being overly self-conscious, constantly fretting about what other people thought of him. Recently he had been promoted. Though he said he had no qualms about the job, the dream—which repeated—was telling him otherwise. In dreamwork, he was able to see that subconsciously, he had fears that other people would think him not qualified and capable.

In the second example, the dreamer had entered into her first serious relationship following her divorce. "G." was her new interest. She interpreted this dream as reflecting her emotional vulnerability, and natural fears about being hurt if she revealed her true self.

Nudity dreams often speak to us about our feelings of, or fears about, our vulnerability, especially when we have embarked on something new in life. Nudity also addresses our openness, sincerity, or naivete. You have nothing to hide, nor do you have the ability to hide anything, when you are nude. Embarrassment over nudity in a dream can reflect embarrassment over something in life: we fear we have "exposed" our flaws or unpreparedness, or that our real self won't measure up to the expectations of others.

Sometimes we find ourselves naked in a dream and are unconcerned about it:

I'm at a train station and go to get on a train. I'm not wearing any clothes. Everyone else is dressed. Nobody pays any attention to me. I don't seem to care that I'm naked. I feel perfectly comfortable.

Here nudity relates to the dreamer's sense of well-being and self-satisfaction: she could be seen for who she really was, without pretense. This dream came after a long period of change and transition, involving remaking her life after loss of her partner, and a radical change of career to what she wanted to do versus what she felt she should do. "I feel I've arrived at long last," the dreamer commented. "I'm at home with who I am in the world." Train stations are crossroads of the world, and represented to her the world at large. She was comfortable "traveling" through life.

In the following dream, another person is nude:

I was driving alone in a car and I was on my way to school, only not high school or college, but elementary school. There was an important lesson for me to learn that day and I was eager to get there. I kept driving from town to town but could not find my school. I remember feeling very anxious at this point, afraid that I might be too late. It was then that I turned to my right and headed back the other direction. When I turned to head back, there was a naked man standing in front of my car. He had gray hair, and I knew he was a radio announcer. He was supposed to be doing a stunt live on the radio, and had a mike in his hand. It was snowing and VERY cold outside. (By the way, I HATE being cold!) He was sliding backward on his feet and facing me, looking at me through the windshield. I was pushing him along. He was supposed to reach his family. I noticed his feet getting redder and then starting to swell, and I wanted to get him there as fast as I could. Then some man on the left side of the road came into sight and he threw a huge pile of snow in the naked man's path; the man was laughing very loudly as if to make fun of him. I started to notice skis on the naked man's feet, but then he started to stumble over the pile of snow . . . that's when I woke up.

The dreamer was a young woman who was feeling stifled in both her marriage and career. She had consciously told herself that she was not ready to make any changes, but her Higher Self kept speaking through dreams to address the need to change. In this dream, her intuition is trying to give her an "elementary" message, that is, something that should be plain and clear to her—but her logical side doesn't want to see it yet. So, in the dream she gets lost and can't find the school (a place where we learn lessons). Her logical side tells her that maybe it's "too late" anyway—a reference to making changes in her life.

The naked man who is the radio announcer also represents her intuition, or Higher Self (announcing a message).

Nudity represents, literally, the "naked truth." He's trying to announce to her the naked truth about her life. He faces, or confronts, her. She doesn't interact with him, just pushes him along backwards. Snow is often a symbol of frozen emotions. The man who throws the snow could be her spouse, or her logical (or masculine) side, which is trying to rationalize everything. He could represent both.

In followup dreamwork, the dreamer did an incubation:

I asked a specific yes-or-no question to my Higher Self before going to sleep in relation to what it is that is right in front of me ("the key, or naked truth"). I did not get a yes-or-no answer, but instead got a clear message that, "You are not allowing yourself to 'see.'" So, I think I need to still let go of some things and open myself up, in other words, be ready. I don't feel so anxious about it today, I'm more excited, actually.

The dreamer was able to move from a state of not being open to change to a willingness to consider change.

Partial Nudity

Also common are dreams in which we suddenly discover we are partially nude. These dreams also can be embarrassing.

I was at my uncle's house in a small Southern city. They were giving a party, and I was invited to it. I had dressed carefully for it, and was talking to some of the guests, when I suddenly discovered that I had forgotten to put on my pants. I wondered what I could do about it. No one seemed to notice it. Without attracting attention, I wondered how I could find my pants and put them on. I did not

find them, and there were guests in every room that I went into. I
woke up, vaguely puzzled as to what I ought to do.[2]

The dreamer attempts to put on a conservative and formal persona (symbolized by the uncle and small Southern city) that he feels will be accepted by others. However, he discovers that what works best is being natural. This is accepted by others wherever he goes—in fact, he cannot put on, or force, the other persona. The dream seems to be saying, "Just be yourself."

In the next example, partial nudity represents a desire to expose feelings and thoughts:

I'm walking through the halls at work with a coworker. My outfit
keeps changing. Then I suddenly discover that I am naked on top. I
try to cover up my breasts with my hands.

The dreamer, a woman, was unhappy at work and was quietly making plans to leave. Her unannounced decision to leave created stress in which she had a difficult time holding her tongue. She wished she could tell others her true but negative feelings and thoughts about the workplace—she wanted to "bare her chest" or be brutally honest. Such an action would not be without consequence, however, symbolized by the embarrassment. She realized that there would be an appropriate time and place to reveal her plans—but also that she needed to give careful consideration to revealing all of her feelings.

SIX

Sex, Marriage and Weddings

Everyone has dreams of a sexual, sensual and erotic nature, and most of us are too embarrassed—or even shocked—by them to talk openly about them. Sometimes sexual dreams are about our unrealized sexual desires and fantasies. Sometimes they concern the sexual nature of, and issues in, our relationships. Sometimes they deal with our feelings about ourselves, such as our attractiveness and desirability, not just in a sexual way but as a whole person. And sometimes sexual dreams are metaphors for other issues involving deep and intimate feelings. Sex and passion in dreams may represent passionate feelings and longings we have about many things in life.

Our sexual dreams differ by gender. Women are more likely to have romantic and passionate sexual dreams in which their lovers are sensitive to their bodies and to arousing them, and spend plenty of time in foreplay. Men are more likely to dream about fast sex and eager sexual partners. Both sexes dream of sexual encounters with celebrities and strangers, but women are more likely than men to dream about sex with former lovers. And both sexes enjoy orgasm during sexual dreams.

After the will to live, the sex drive is the most powerful force in life; thus it's not surprising that sex colors much of our dreaming. Rather than shy away from our sexual dreams, we should examine them for their wisdom and messages.

Sex and Intimacy

Sex in dreams is often less inhibited than in waking life. Dreams liberate us sexually. We do provocative things we ordinarily would not do; we have sex with strangers; we have casual sex. Dream sex does not—and should not—encourage us to loosen our morals and act irresponsibly, but it does give us a certain freedom to experiment.

Sometimes highly erotic dreams encourage us to be more open with our waking life partners. The dreamer of the following example was too "uptight" in bed, according to her husband. One night she had this dream:

R. and I are in bed making love. Suddenly I feel very sexy, almost animalistic. I make love in a way I never have before. R. is very pleased and responds to my brazen behavior. It's the best sex I've ever had.

This dream was embarrassing to the dreamer, who would "never behave that way." Nonetheless, the pleasure she experienced, as well as the response of her husband, encouraged her to be bolder in their lovemaking. She did not go to the extremes of the dream, but did allow herself to be more open and experimental.

CLOSURE FOR OLD LOVE

As mentioned, women more than men dream of old lovers. Lovers from the past can become idealized in a romantic way, especially if we have not lived with them on an intimate basis as a spouse. Living with someone day to day reveals faults and shortcomings in even the best of partners. Enduring love requires acceptance, patience, honesty and flexibility. The highs of initial intense and consuming passion cannot be sustained in a long-term relationship. Old lovers in dreams can symbolize the ideals of passion without the attendant responsibilities of commitment in daily life.

The following dream about a previous boyfriend came unexpectedly, long after the relationship was over. The dreamer had had an intense attraction to the man and genuinely believed he was "the one." They dated, but he always seemed emotionally distant. Though she was more than willing to have sex, he never went beyond kissing and fondling. She tried to give him all the right signals, but he didn't pick up on them. The subject of sex was never discussed.

She was frustrated that the relationship wouldn't catch fire. Then he abruptly dropped out of her life. Much later, she learned through gossip that he most likely had an impotency problem, which explained to her his unassertive sexual behavior. For a long time, she thought about him and what might have been. Then, years later, long after he had passed from daily thought, he appeared in a lucid dream:

I go to a convention where I run into B. It has been years, and to my happy surprise, he is glad to see me. We talk briefly and I tell him of my travel plans. He asks what I've been doing and is genuinely interested in what I have to say. The conversation is short and he seems elusive. This time, though, something is different—there is a spark in his eye. I think, "maybe." I go to my hotel room and go to bed. Suddenly he is there in bed and we make love for the first time ever. I am supremely happy, for B. is very tender and passionate. Real emotion behind it. I cancel my trip and stay at the convention, and the affair grows. He is no longer ice, but truly cares. I can hardly believe it and wonder if we will marry. I know this is a dream and we must work this out between us.

B. tells me for the first time ever how much he loves me and he has always loved me. I tell him I love him, too. We have this talk on the rocky beach of a glistening sea. It is somewhere in the north and seems cool, though others are sitting out on beach chairs. The water is deep, dark blue. Across the bay is a beautiful range of snow-capped mountains.

At this point, I expect to resolve things, like we acknowledge our feelings and say "but not in this life" or something like that. But the dream begins to come apart—I get distracted thinking about finally being in this situation—and I lose it. For a moment, though, I experienced a warmth and happiness I don't ever remember having before in a dream.

The dream expresses her old deep longing for a passionate romance, one that she once fantasized would develop between her and B. As a dream lover, he satisfies the fantasy where he failed in waking life. There is open acknowledgment of love, something else that never really occurred. And, there is a soul-satisfying baring of the heart set against a backdrop of nature. The sea represents emotions. The rocky beach is a symbol of the foundation of the relationship. The distant mountains represent distant, other goals. The cool environment is tempering.

Like a shopping mall, a convention represents choices. It also represents lessons and learning, for we go to conventions to acquire information, experience and skills. The drama is set in a place of choices and learning.

Though the frank talk doesn't have quite the completion the dreamer hoped for, there is nonetheless the feeling in the dream of closure, and that a relationship is not meant "in this life." The dreamer felt strongly that the dream enabled her to close her emotional books on the relationship and leave it not as a frustrated memory, but as a pleasant memory.

SEXUAL AND OTHER PROBLEMS

A woman who was losing sexual interest in her husband had this dream:

I am engaged to K. I am not particularly attracted to him or enthused about it, but I go along with it. We are living in a dorm of single men and women while we try to save enough money to buy a house. I wonder why I have committed to a recovering alcoholic who could slide back on the bottle any day. But, he's a big guy and I feel he will protect me. He complains, however, about my lack of interest in touching him intimately, so I do so in a perfunctory way.

K. was a man she knew only slightly. Her marriage was in trouble. Her husband drank too much and denied that he had a problem. They had many fights, usually started from a temper flare-up of his after he had been drinking. When he was angry, he was verbally abusive, and called her foul names. She felt betrayed at a deep level of being. He was not big physically, but he was big financially. This is the protection the dreamer felt in the dream: money would protect her from the world and even from her own emotions. Their sex life had deteriorated, and it was an effort for her to engage in sex. She often thought about divorce, but "went along" with staying married because it seemed easier than going through a breakup.

She felt the dormitory in the dream represented their lack of intimacy, for there is no intimacy in a dorm; they offer no privacy and are rather sterile. The single men and women represented her emotional ambivalence—she was not attached emotionally to her husband, or to anything. Saving money to buy a house represented to her a desire to have a new or safe lifestyle. As a couple, they were emotionally bankrupt, and didn't have what it took for a healthy relationship.

K. was a large man physically, and was a recovering alcoholic. He was divorced and lived alone. The dreamer felt that because he no longer drank, he represented a hope to her that her own husband would also quit.

THWARTED OR INTERRUPTED SEX

Dreams of wanting to have sex, or starting to have sex, only to be interrupted or thwarted often represent something that is interfering in the intimate bonding of the partners. Such obstacles could be other people who are allowed to be too much a part of the relationship (parents, family members, ex-lovers) or distractions on the part of one of the partners, such as job or substance abuse. Interference builds up resentment in the other partner.

I have this recurring dream that when I go to get in bed with my husband, a man with a hunting rifle suddenly shows up in the bedroom. I'm afraid he is going to kill my husband.

The dreamer realized that the man represented her husband's avid interest in hunting. Every hunting season, he would take frequent trips into the woods with several male companions. When he was not hunting, he spent a lot of his spare time with his hunting buddies. The wife resented the time spent away from home. She felt like a "hunting widow," and that his interest in hunting was threatening to kill their intimacy.

The next dream has a common theme of sex ruined by the ultimate authority figures, parents.

D. and I are living with his parents, who sleep in the same room. Ruins sex. Drives me nuts. In the living room, I want to read, but none of the lights work. Can't get light to shed on something, it seems. This has been the status quo with his parents for two years and I tell D. we must do something because I've had it.

The dreamer had a difficult relationship with her in-laws, mirrored starkly in the dream. She felt they meddled in her marriage with her husband, represented by the sharing of intimate space and being an obstacle to sex. In the living room, the focal point of a home and a marriage, she tries to bury herself in reading, but none of the lights can be turned on. In the dream, she tells her husband about her frustrations—something she had not done in real life.

The dream literally turned on a light for the dreamer. She realized that there was nothing to be gained by ignoring the situation and keeping silent—her frustrations were mounting. She needed to have a talk with her husband, especially before her irritation exploded in an angry outburst that would cause a lot of damage.

The dream also addressed another issue that was separate from the in-laws. The dream in-laws are authority figures that make sure there will be no pleasure in sex. This symbolized the dreamer's own inner killjoy authority. She had learned from her mother, mostly by inference, that sex was dirty and not to be enjoyed.

SEX WITH A CELEBRITY

Like other dreams involving our encounters with celebrities and important persons, sex with celebrities can represent our desire to be loved and feel important:

I am at an airport, coming home from a conference or business meeting, and I meet Robin Williams, who is also returning home. Somehow we hit it off and he is very friendly to me. Though other people recognize him, no one seems to dare to approach him except me.

We are both waiting. My luggage has been lost and is being returned to me. He is waiting for his limo service. We chat a bit (can't remember about what). Then I am given back my luggage, which is my small black carry-on bag on wheels. He is notified that his ride is ready. He offers me a ride home. I decide to take it. We get in an open Jeep, which he drives. Things are going so well that

I want to ask him out. I start to say, "Would it be too forward if . . ."
and he simultaneously starts to say the same thing. We laugh. He
invites me to have dinner at his house. I accept, very happy.

When we get to his house, I see grounds which are landscaped
with beautiful fountains and gardens. I feel very attracted to Robin
and know that he is attracted to me, too. He picks me up and carries
me into the house, and upstairs to his bedroom. I am tingling with
electricity. We make passionate love on a big bed.

The dreamer associated actor and comedian Robin Williams with fun, humor, boldness and risk-taking. Her own
sense of identity, represented by the lost and small black
bag, reveals how she thinks about herself. She desires to be
more noticeable, more attractive, and more open, like the
Jeep that Williams drives home. The lush and beautiful gardens add to the sensuality, and also express the deep inner
desire of the dreamer to be appreciated as beautiful and
sensual.

Sometimes characteristics or behavior of the dream celebrity lover remind us of our own partner. Or, they can
express our wishes for what we would like in a partner.

FORCED SEX

Dreams of rape and forced, unpleasant sex are seldom
reported by men, but are reported by many women. These
themes can represent attitudes of smoldering resentment
toward a spouse or partner ("I resent having to have sex
with you because of how you've hurt me"). Abused women
are the most likely to have sexual dreams in which they are
threatened or harmed, or in which sex is painful and humiliating.

Forced sex dreams can also serve as metaphors for having to do some task or obligation that the dreamer finds very unpleasant or humiliating, or which violates ethics, standards or morals, such as in this example:

I am sleeping in my bed when two thugs break in and attack me. They tie me up in a corner and I know they intend to rape me.

The dreamer argued frequently with her husband. The fights never became physical, but they involved verbal abuse that always deeply wounded the dreamer. When the fight was over, she wanted time to withdraw and collect herself, but her husband expected her to be "normal" again and have sex as though nothing were wrong. She felt emotionally violated by this.

In the next dream, the threat of forced sex serves as a metaphor for an unpleasant choice in the life of the dreamer:

I am in my hotel room, only it is much larger. I am in bed asleep. As I wake up, I realize someone else is there. A man pulls back the covers. It is someone I have met the day before, one of twins. He is handsome and well-built with dark hair, a hairy chest and black-rimmed glasses. He wears only a pair of black bikini underpants (the style for men). I am on my back and he gets on top of me, straddling. I tell him no, go away, I am not interested, I am married and very loyal to my husband. He thinks he can persuade me to have sex with him.

Just then the conference organizer comes in. He says, "I see what you have been doing" in a disapproving voice. I say, "No, it's not like that," and make the man get off. I will explain to the organizer later. The man is angry and says he will get back at me.

The dreamer was attending a conference when she had this dream, and the conference provides some day residue. The sexual threat is a metaphor for something that threatens the dreamer on an intimate, or deeply personal, basis. It concerned a possible course of action she did not want to take, but for various reasons felt obliged to. The matter did not concern her marriage, but her career. The dream showed her how strong was her negative emotion reaction. The conference organizer is her inner authority, which shows disapproval. The angry man is her fear that she would anger others if she did not take the unwanted course of action.

A sexual theme concerned a career matter for another dreamer in the next example:

I am having an affair with E. We are in his house, which is quite luxurious and very ornately decorated. Every chance we have to be alone, we sneak these passionate embraces and the sweetest, passionate kisses. There is the implication that we are sexually involved, but no sex takes place in the dream.

E. is married to a very unattractive woman. She is short, squat and ugly, with long brown hair cut in a page boy. She reminds me of these old drawings I saw from Alice in Wonderland *of the Queen. I am concerned about his wife finding out about us, as we take risks. But the satisfaction of the physical contact with E. is too compelling. There seems to be some understanding or discussion between us of the consequences. If she finds out, she will throw him out. A couple of times, I think she sees us—we are not fast enough to break our embrace. But there is no confrontation.*

The dreamer, a woman, knew E. He was a professional acquaintance who lived some distance away. He was not someone to whom she was sexually attracted. She was happily married. What's more, she hadn't seen or spoken to E. for more than three years, since they last met at a conference. She had met his wife, who was an attractive woman, not anything like the dream wife.

The dreamer did not think that the dream was compensatory in terms of affection. She and her husband shared a warm, affectionate and sexual relationship. "There's something about E. that I want, but I don't know what it is," she said.

After group dreamwork, the dreamer had a deep intuitive hit: the dream was about being valued professionally. E. was very successful, regarded as an authority in his field (his "house" in the dream). At the conference where they'd last met, he was indeed a star. The dreamer worked in the same field. Though she professed that she felt competent and knew her work was excellent, she felt that others didn't recognize her for her true worth. She did not get the same recognition that he did.

This dream helped her to face two important truths about herself. The first was that she still had an underlying self-confidence issue, despite what she professed to others. She wasn't sure in the deep center of her being that she really *was* as great as she said. The second truth concerned risk-taking. She was conservative and played it safe. E., on the other hand, was a maverick who took risks. As she put it, E. was someone who "got the glory" while she was someone who "did all the real work."

The unattractive wife was that part of her that literally was "married" to her, and which didn't want to credit or acknowledge her talent and success. The wife played a role similar to the dreamer's mother, who always minimized her daughter's aspirations and accomplishments. This negative mother aspect made no direct confrontation, but preferred to create tension behind the scenes, just as in the dream— like a guerilla who builds up fear and tension over the timing and place of the next strike. The dream wife is ready to "throw out" any glimmers of success.

The dreamer developed an action plan from this dream. First and foremost was to not minimize her successes and accomplishments, but to *feel* her own success, and know that it was valid, no matter what the feedback. Public approval is not necessarily a measure of success. For example, some of the greatest artists in history are people who were not appreciated in their time.

This does not mean that we should disregard contemporary standards for success. We live in a world where recognition is important. However, many people produce high-quality work without becoming superstars. The true key to happiness in life lies in your own satisfaction in what you do, not in the approval of others.

The second part of the dreamer's plan of action was to stop looking to others for validation or approval. This is distinctly different from her first action, to feel her own success. One can experience one's own success, but still want others to see it and validate it. This sets up an endless search for validation and approval. As the dreamer put it, "There's always something I'm missing in order to feel I've finally arrived."

The third part of the dreamer's plan was to stop comparing herself to others. Success for one person does not necessarily apply to another.

The older we get, the more we dream about our attractiveness. Women who are reaching midlife especially worry that they are losing their desirability. Women have been conditioned by advertising, the media and social behavior that men—no matter what their age and shape—always prefer young women.

I dreamed that my husband was having an affair with a woman who is a friend of mine. I found them in my house, kissing passionately. It made me feel sick.

The emotions were so intense in this dream that the dreamer wondered if she had received a warning that her husband really was having an affair with her friend. Her husband, however, was quite devoted to her, and they enjoyed a good relationship. There were no outward signs that anything was amiss. The dreamer acknowledged that she often worried that she wouldn't remain interesting and attractive enough to keep her husband faithful to her. The dream reflected these anxieties. The woman friend represented traits desired by the wife. The dream helped the wife to realize that her fears were unfounded, but she needed to bolster her self-esteem.

A woman who felt her husband was losing interest in her had this dream:

I am mistress of a large, wealthy household. I cruelly inform one of the young kitchen help that my husband has no particular feelings for her as she fancies he does, but he falls for all young girls. She

is devastated. He is furious that I have told her. I am indignant. 83
Humiliated, she leaves.

DREAMSPEAK

The dreamer is both the older woman and the young kitchen help. In waking life, the dreamer enjoyed a comfortable lifestyle, but felt emotionally impoverished and fearful of her husband's waning interest in favor of younger women. Emotionally, she felt she had no option but to leave.

INFIDELITY WARNINGS

In exceptional cases, dreams about infidelity really are warnings about infidelity in waking life. For example, a woman dreams her husband is having an affair with a neighbor. She relates it to her husband, who dismisses it as "a silly dream." Later, the wife discovers information validating the dream. In her book *Sexual Dreams*, Gayle Delaney relates the case of a woman who, with her husband, gave many large dinner parties. One night she dreamed that they gave a dinner party, and the bread basket was passed around just to the women. When it got to her, she saw that it contained not bread but her husband's penis. It turned out that her husband had had sex with many of the women who had attended their dinner parties. The woman divorced him.

In such cases, the dreamer has probably already received subtle (or even obvious) signs about the infidelity, but has chosen to ignore them. Or, the dreamer's intuition picks up signals that aren't consciously acknowledged. Sexual involvement is one of the hardest things to hide. The electricity that sparks between lovers registers on others, whether they look for it or not.

If you have a dream involving the infidelity of your partner, do not quickly jump to conclusions, however. First see how the dream relates to yourself and your emotions.

PROSTITUTES AND "OTHER WOMEN"

When women dream about prostitutes and "other women," they may be dreaming about their own repressed sexuality. If sexuality is denied or ignored, it can find expression in extremes in dreams as a very earthy, very sexual woman. Such a figure is a shadow—a repressed part of one's self that Jung succinctly defined as "the thing a person has no wish to be." Shadow figures often take on a threatening or undesirable presence:

> My husband is having an affair with another woman. She comes to my house to confront me. She is dark-haired and voluptuous, and dressed very provocatively. She seems totally sexual in a way that I am not. I coolly demand that she stop seeing my husband. She starts following me around the house, screaming at me that I wouldn't be losing my husband if I were more like her. I try to ignore her and then I start screaming back at her. I grab her and shake her real hard. Then I grab a pair of scissors and just cut her up like a paper doll.

This was a nightmare for the dreamer, and occurred close to the end of her marriage. As the marriage was unraveling, sex had dwindled to nothing. The voluptuous "other woman" in the dream is the sexual side of the dreamer longing to be expressed. The other woman also represents what is threatening the marriage—which was not infidelity but a breakdown of a variety of factors. The dreamer tries to reject her sexual side and even cut it out of her life.

SEX WITH AN INAPPROPRIATE PERSON

A common sexual dream is to be passionate or sexual with a family member (incest) or with a platonic friend or coworker, or someone you know but to whom you have no attraction whatsoever. These dreams are puzzling, embarrassing and shocking.

Sometimes incestuous dreams do relate to real incest or the threat of incest earlier in life. More often, such dreams are speaking in metaphors about qualities we see in ourselves or others with whom we are involved intimately.

A woman who worked in middle management in a large corporation dreamed of having passionate embraces and kisses with a coworker, a manager in another department. She knew the man only slightly. She liked and respected him, but had no attraction to him. Asked what he represented, she answered that she liked his sense of humor and easygoing manner. She realized she wished her own husband were more easygoing and not so heavy-handed.

Dreams of sex with parents or siblings can relate to qualities by association as well. We usually do select partners who remind us of our parents or who repeat parental behaviors that we unconsciously seek.

INNER BALANCE

Passionate and harmonious love sometimes symbolizes an inner harmony achieved within the dreamer. If one's masculine and feminine natures (the animus and the anima) are balanced and in harmony with each other, they are intimately entwined as lovers:

I dream of a lake with Chillon Castle beside it in Switzerland. The scene is very, very beautiful, magical and serene, very peaceful. (Chillon is a castle I have always loved in Switzerland, "Le Chateau de Chillon.")

On the lake is a glowing white ball which looks like a crystal bubble. This ball is floating on the surface of the lake, and inside the ball, each time I look during the night, are white (marble or alabaster-looking) Lovers. The Lovers are entwined in an embrace like Rodin's "Lovers," yet their physical bodies look like the white Lover statues G. and B. and I saw on the Gulf of Finland on our walk.

For the dreamer, this dream brought great healing energy, not only about relationships but about her inner balance of masculine and feminine. Deep inside, we both have a masculine side and a feminine side, both of which are important to our well-being. When both work in harmony and balance, they can appear in dreams as lovers, testifying to a deep interconnection within us.

The dream also had meaning for the dreamer's new relationship with a man who was to become an emotional support for her.

The lake symbolizes calm emotions (there are no upsetting waves), and the crystal ball that contains the lovers seems idealized and magical—a look into the future.

The dreamer wrote in her journal:

I was thrilled by this dream, because the Lovers inside of the crystal ball floating on the serene lake beside Chillon Castle looked very much like the Lovers I had seen at the deserted cafe on our walk beside the Gulf of Finland. But in this dream those Lovers were now entwined like Rodin's Lovers. And they were white as those Lovers were on the beach and on Rodin's picture, which I have now in almost every room in my house. I brought a postcard home from Switzerland with the picture of these Lovers on it.

In my life I now had communications with many wonderful men who were all married. They were like members of my "Roundtable," all very respectful of me, all very loving of me, and all very appreciative of me, like my dearest friends, all men I could have fallen deeply in love with if they were not married.

So instead they all became dear friends of mine. One I did fall in love with and he with me, but our agreement was that we would be dear friends, and could be nothing else due to his commitments, which I very much honor. But this man has helped (as my platonic friend) balance my inner male with my inner female.

The Lovers on the Lake remind me of the union I have achieved internally and externally in terms of balance and harmony since meeting these wonderful men, and having their love and respect enter my life.

In my past I have been very confused with men, and often been abused or neglected or invalidated by the ones with whom I allowed myself to be involved. So after a long period of celibacy to heal, these dreams were very supportive, that I was healing! My Inner Male and Inner Female seem to be coming into harmony and balance, so that both sides can support me.

OTHER SEXUAL IMAGES

Many dreams not overtly sexual in content are nonetheless about sex, such as this dream:

F. and I are asleep in our house. I awaken in the middle of the night and somehow know that the power has gone out. I wake up

F., who gets up to go down into the basement to investigate the furnace. He takes a flashlight.

The dreamer, divorced, was in a new and passionate relationship. For the last several years of her marriage she had not had sex with her husband. Here the furnace and flashlight have obvious Freudian female and male connotations. The power going out of the furnace refers to her sexually lifeless former marriage. In fact, the dreamer often remarked that she felt her "pilot light" as a woman had gone out. Her new partner has the solution.

Sexual meaning can be found in many dream images. For example, another woman who was in a new and passionate relationship dreamed of the desire to clean her house. With great energy, she began vacuuming her rug. The rug and vacuum cleaner are sexual symbols like the furnace and flashlight (interestingly, vacuum cleaners appear often as phallic symbols in sexual message dreams). Cleaning her house represented the new energy she felt coming into her life—it was time to get rid of old stuff.

Fire and electricity appear as symbols of intense passion in many sexual dreams:

M. and I are at a resort. He builds a fire and I go to bed. He comes to give me a massage. The fire burns the apartment.

Sexual messages also are contained in slang terms for body parts and sex acts, and in plays on words. Wild animals—especially those that chase us or run out of control— can symbolize sexuality that seeks to break free.

Marriage and wedding dreams are related to sex and intimacy dreams, for they concern the most intimate and personal parts of life. Marriage dreams can reflect the state of our real marriage, as in this dream:

> I dreamed we were giving an anniversary dinner, because of the tenth anniversary of our marriage. My little daughter sat at one end of the table, and I at the other. In addition to my son, a number of my friends and their wives were present, and several other guests. The maid served an excellent meal. . . . The dream shifted; the adults played bridge. There would have been a person missing, since the three couples present consisted of husbands and wives, if an unmarried friend of mine had not dropped in, just as we were about to play. I woke up, saying to myself what a glorious evening it had been.[1]

The significance of this dream is what is missing from it: the dreamer's wife is not present. The anniversary party is attended by other family and friends of the husband. It is enjoyed immensely by the husband, despite the absence of the wife. The husband admitted that he and his wife had not been on good terms. The dream reveals honest emotions: life goes on quite pleasantly without her. The bridge game can also be seen as a symbol of a bridge to a new life, formed by friends, including an unmarried one.

Marriage dreams also symbolize things to which we are committed, and things to which we have bound ourselves, for better or for worse:

Somehow I find myself agreeing to marry P., even though I am not attracted to him and know my life will suffer as a result. Other people seem to urge me to do this, and I go along with it, even though I know it is not in my best interests. I am consigning myself to a life of poverty.

In waking life, P. was a friend with whom the dreamer had never had any romantic involvement, and both were married to other persons. P. was somewhat unkempt in appearance and was always struggling for money. In the dream, P. represented issues the dreamer was struggling with, and had been struggling with for many years. She had a hard time managing her money. She liked to keep up appearances and spent money freely. She was always in debt, and always vowing to get out of debt—but something always prompted her to spend money again. She had a great fear of being poor.

The dreamer felt that P. represented her preoccupation with appearances—her fear of looking and being poor—as well as her spending habits, which jeopardized her security. She was voluntarily married to behavior that would keep her struggling for money. The other people in the dream, who encourage the marriage, represented the temptations to keep spending money.

Wedding dreams can be perplexing, especially if no wedding plans are in the offing in life, or we have not recently married, or we are not leaving a marriage. Many wedding dreams are not about relationships at all. Weddings are symbols of making a commitment to something that is very important to the dreamer. They inaugurate a totally new way of life. Most of us would not marry unless we were absolutely certain of ourselves. Yet we make many commitments in life—to people, jobs, organizations and projects—without enthusiasm, because we feel we ought to do so. Consider the following dream:

I was getting married to a man I hardly knew. I am not sure why we were getting married. I was not excited. I felt rather matter-of-fact in the dream. We had a big reception before getting married. I was in my formal wedding dress and we sat at a head table (even though we weren't married yet). We did not visit any of the other tables at the reception (I guess, because we were not married). As the night progressed it slipped away and we never did get around to getting married. I saw my fiance with another woman and wondered why they weren't getting married; they seemed perfect for each other. They seemed in love. In fact, I wanted to tell them to get married and wasn't upset at all. In another scene we were in a house and we went to the basement. A guest was sleeping on a mattress on the floor. We went to the basement to get some clean laundry.

Before going to the basement I had been in a cozy parlor visiting with the man (fiance) and the woman. I was wondering why we were supposed to marry. It didn't seem logical when they got along so well. I think I was relieved.

The dreamer recognized this dream as a message about her career. Her intuition was telling her not to "marry," or commit herself, to something she was not certain was right for her. "This dream was about being my authentic self and not doing anything that I can't put my heart and soul into," she said. "I need to listen to my emotional guidance." A key to this dream is the sleeping guest in the basement, a signal to look within for a sleeping truth about what she really wanted to do.

The next wedding dream deals with the dreamer's self-image:

> I beg my ex-husband to marry me again, but he rejects me, telling me he is in love with someone else and they are going to be married. He invites me to the wedding. When I go, I am shocked to discover how ugly and unattractive the bride is. She is so masculine that she even has somewhat of a beard! I am amazed that he would be attracted to her when I am so much more appealing.

The dreamer's second marriage was rocky, and she did entertain fantasies about reuniting with her first husband. Her self-esteem was very low, symbolized by the ugly, masculine bride who beats her out of the competition for the affections of the first husband. The ugly bride also symbolized the dreamer's feelings about herself as a sexual being. She felt very unattractive to her second husband.

The next dream concerns romantic relationships:

> I dreamed that a girl friend came to see me all dressed up in lavender with a bridesmaid's hat and about to be married. I sharply discounted the marriage. I seemed to be sitting all hunched up and suffering from the close air of the room. I kept turning the radiator off and on until another girl came in and informed me that I had a hole in the heel of my stocking—and this to me who am the soul of neatness.[2]

The dreamer was a successful career woman who had difficulty forming close friendships with others, both men and women. She was friendly, even encouraging, toward men, but if they became too romantic or sexual, her behavior turned cold and mean, often to the destruction of the relationship. The girl friend in the dream is that part of her that longed for an emotionally intimate relationship—but she was always a bridesmaid, never the bride. Another part of her tried to convince her that such a thing was worthless. The on and off radiator symbolizes both her behavior toward men and her own uncertain sexuality. This conflict is the one hole in her otherwise perfectly groomed world. The heel also calls to mind the Achilles' heel—one's point of greatest weakness or vulnerability.

Our sexuality is intimately connected to everything in life: self-esteem, success in relationships, ability to express emotions, ability to give and receive love, appreciation of beauty and creative expression. Dreams with strong sexual content are good barometers of how well we are doing and what needs to be changed.

SEVEN

Money, Valuables and Treasures

It's tempting to think that dreams of finding money, valuables and treasure are prophetic indicators of future wealth. That's not impossible, but most dreams about money and valuables concern our anxieties, values and spending habits—as well as our inner wealth of spiritual values, talents and self-esteem.

WISH FULFILLMENTS

If we're suffering from financial lack, we may have wish-fulfillment dreams in which we suddenly find or receive large sums of money or other riches, as in the following two examples:

*I dreamed that the boyfriend I go with asked me to marry him.
We were married, and for our honeymoon we had a trip around the
world. When we got back, he bought a wonderful house in the country. I had all the money I wanted to buy things with, jewels, beautiful
dresses, automobiles and everything.*[1]

The reality of the situation was that both the dreamer
and her boyfriend were out of work and had very little
money.

*I dreamed that my father, who left my mother three years ago,
came back to the house with a bag over his shoulder. The bag contained $3,000, which he had won in a lottery. We were all very
happy.*[2]

The abandoned family did not know the whereabouts of
the father and was in trouble financially. The dream expressed a wish for the father to return home, and for the
financial pressure to be eased. The image of the father appearing with a bag over his shoulder is reminiscent of Santa
Claus, which underscores the fantasy of the wish. Money
won in a lottery symbolizes a magical, effortless and instant
solution to the problem.

MONEY WORRIES

Anxieties about money and debt and "having enough"
are often reflected in dreams in which we lose our wallets
or purses, or we are robbed. The thief, whether known or
invisible, can represent the person or situation that is "robbing" the dreamer of financial security. The true thief is

likely to be the dreamer, whose bad spending and saving habits or bad financial decisions have caused the drain.

I am at a conference at Easter time. One of our events is attending a special Easter service at a local Russian Orthodox Church. The group goes off to walk to the church. We have placed all of our personal belongings in a big room. I am still in the room checking to see that my things are okay. There is a strange red-haired man sorting through things. He picks up a little black belly bag, opens it and takes out a handful of change. "It's amazing what people leave in these things," he says as he tosses the bag onto a pile of clothing. I am shocked to recognize my own belly bag, and it dawns on me that this man is a thief. "That's my bag and you have just taken my money!" I say sternly. "I want it back." He looks chagrined to be caught and digs in his front pocket. He hands me a quarter and some pennies. "I had more than this!" I say. The man bolts. I run outside and wave at the group, now across the street. "Thief, thief!" I shout at the fleeing man, but he gets away.

I really want to go to the church service, and the rest of the group seems to think the security problem is solved. We go to the church, an old building with lots of ornate wood and an elaborate staircase that winds down and down. The service is in a little room at the bottom.

As the group descends the staircase, I decide to pass on the service and return to the room with our belongings. There is nothing to prevent the man from returning while everybody is gone.

When I get back to the room, I see that someone has already been there and stolen things. There is a black purse that resembles mine. I open it and discover everything has been taken. I fear the worst. Then I find my own purse. I am relieved to discover that everything is still inside: a wallet with lots of money, my calendar and other things. Somehow the thief took everybody else's valuables but left mine. I think, "I still have my money," or "I still have every- 97

thing that is mine."

DREAMSPEAK

The dreamer was indeed the cause of her own financial problems through reckless spending. She was in a great deal of anxiety over how she was going to pay off a large credit debt. The dream was reassuring to her, telling her that she still had the resources—determination, discipline and so on—to stay solvent. She also realized that she still had what really mattered more than money: health, a good relationship, a home and family.

An unexplored part of the dream is the church service at the bottom of a winding staircase. Perhaps answers to her financial predicament could be found through innerwork of a spiritual nature.

Another dreamer in a similar situation had this dream:

I am about to go on a trip with a station wagon–load of women. They seem to be people I met during a conference. Everyone is waiting on me, and I suddenly discover that my wallet is gone. I had been walking through a big store with it in my hip pocket, and someone stole it. Fortunately, I had taken all the cash out, and I still had a big stack of money. But my driver's license and credit cards are gone. Now I won't be able to charge anything and get frequent flyer miles. Also, I must now deal with reporting stolen cards and getting a new license. Everyone is getting impatient.

The dreamer understood the message immediately upon awakening: it was about her perpetual problem of running up credit card debt. Her identity is tied up in money, symbolized by her wallet full of credit cards and her driver's license identification. She realized that she was the true thief. By not being able to manage her spending, she was robbing herself and her family. At the point of the dream, she hadn't lost everything—she still had money left. She realized she would have to stop her careless spending, or else all of her resources would indeed be "stolen."

Resentment toward others who have more wealth is mirrored in the next dream:

Some wealthy people are being held captive. I seem to be one of the captors. I act violently and aggressively toward an older wealthy woman, essentially ripping her apart like a doll with scissors and knives.

"Money is turning me into a monster," the dreamer noted in her dream journal. More specifically, her obsession with becoming wealthy was the culprit. The scissors and knives, cutting instruments, are symbols of the need to cut this behavior from her life, before it ripped her apart.

DAMAGED VALUABLES

Valuables that are lost or damaged may be symbols of something else—such as a once-valued relationship—that has lost its luster:

H. and I are somewhere in Canada and are in a beautiful old city with lots of water, almost like canals. We go out with another couple in their boat for sightseeing. We dock the boat and get off to go into town. There is a big red-brick castle with slim turrets on a hill.

I realize I forgot my watch and rings and we have to go back to the boat. I find them and put on the watch and wedding ring, which is uncomfortable. I look down and see that it has been mashed, like

it's been stepped on, and it is bent and nearly broken through. I cry.
I say I will have to get a new ring, but H. says we can't afford it if
we are going to move.

The dreamer's marriage was deteriorating. The beautiful old city represented happier times, and the red-brick castle in the distance was the potential for renewal. The large amount of water (emotions) was divided into many choices (canals). The damaged and uncomfortable wedding ring spoke dramatically to the dreamer about the state of the relationship. The watch told her it was time to do something. The dream told her of her true willingness to make changes (get a new ring), but she was uncertain about her husband's true feelings. The dream helped her to move out of an emotional limbo and initiate an effort to rebuild her marriage.

FAIR COMPENSATION

The dreamer in the next case had this dream about a year after she had left a salaried job and started her own public relations consulting business:

I am doing volunteer work for some women's organization. They
are going out of business, so I will have no more work from them.
They have no resources. I find out that they went to N. and asked
him for advice. He gave them some, but it was nothing important.
Then he insisted on getting paid a fee. He told them to take stock
of their inventory of cans of motor oil, and give him 10 percent.

I go to him, angry that he is extracting a fee from them when he
did nothing to help. He says he has to get paid something for his

work. I wonder, why did they pay him when they have not paid me anything?

N. was a man she knew from her professional life, also a self-employed public relations consultant, whom she perceived was doing much better than she with far less effort. After a year in business, the dreamer felt frustrated over her billings. It seemed she was always agreeing to work for a greatly reduced fee in order to get business. She could not seem to persuade people that she was worth higher fees. In fact, sometimes she felt as though she might as well work for nothing—like a volunteer. N., on the other hand, always seemed to be "well oiled."

In the dream, N. holds his ground about receiving a fee. To the dreamer, he was a symbol of her desire to be well compensated. The dream's message to her was about her need to know her own worth and hold to that when negotiating work.

"I hadn't turned down jobs even when the fees were low because I felt I couldn't afford to say no," the dreamer said. "I thought my work would prove itself and lead to better fees. Instead, people kept expecting me to work for the same low rates." The dream's women's organization that goes out of business represented the dreamer's draining stress and worry that she would herself go out of business.

It took some courage, but the dreamer starting turning down low-paying jobs. She set what she considered to be a fair value on her services, and made some guidelines for herself about her range of negotiation. Her fees and selectivity raised her value in the marketplace. "It's all a matter of perception," she said.

Sometimes money represents something else of value to the dreamer, such as time, commitment and effort—one's personal resources.

A red-haired young man tries to explain to me how much financial trouble he is in. He tells me he has gotten a loan, and shows me the papers. He wants me to explain the terms to him. I look at them and exclaim, "Well, you've agreed to pay an interest rate of 110 percent!" He is crestfallen. "That won't do," he says.

The dreamer, a woman, had been asked to take on a volunteer project. She had little interest in it, but felt she could not say no, despite the commitment it would require in time and energy—and possibly money out of her own pocket. The young man in the dream represents her logical side, who tries to explain her inner balance sheet is in the red. The 110 percent interest rate reflects a complaint the dreamer was nursing: "It looks like I am going to have to give 110 percent of myself if I'm going to get this done and do everything else too!" The young man's proclamation, "That won't do," is a message to the dreamer that this project truly is not in her best interests. Though it was difficult for her, the dreamer bowed out of the project, saying she had overestimated the time she would have available.

It was a valuable lesson. Too often, we automatically say yes to requests because we don't want to disappoint people, don't want them to think ill of us, or sincerely would like to be helpful. Saying yes to requests gains us the approval of others—or so we think. In fact, people have more respect for individuals who know their limits and boundaries. Some even secretly envy those who have the courage to say no. We will not be disliked if we sometimes say no.

Spiritual Value of Treasures

Many dreams dealing with money, valuables and treasure are not addressing our financial affairs and values, but are addressing spiritual values: love, self-worth, purpose in life, a sense of connection to everything, virtues and so on. Such things carry no price tags, for they are beyond price. These dreams are vivid and emotional, retaining a transformative power that lasts for years. They help to awaken us to a deeper meaning in life that transcends the ups and downs of daily concerns.

The spiritual symbolism of treasures appears in many myths. In Tibetan Buddhist mythology, there is a place of great mystery and magic known as Shambhala. The name Shambhala is Sanskrit and means "the Source of All Happiness." The journey to find Shambhala is a metaphor for our spiritual journey to find the Self—the journey that each of us makes through life.

Shambhala is a land of peace and contentment, where enlightened inhabitants are free from disease, illness, vice, poverty and old age. It is filled with wonderful, magical fruit trees and treasures of precious metals and gems. The kingdom is protected from contamination by the outer world, represented in myth by two rings of snowy mountains and heavy mists. It lies like the jewel in the heart of an eight-petalled lotus. Only the most pure and worthy find it and recognize it, usually after a long and arduous journey.

There are two ways to find Shambhala. The first is through the spiritual search. The seeker is called through dreams and visions in which the mists clear and the kingdom is glimpsed. The seeker then must figure out on his own how to get there. The journey is fraught with perils. The terrain is rough, and the traveler is beset by temptations that come in the form of people who try to lure him off the path. He is attacked by his lower nature in the form of beasts and demons. If all those obstacles are overcome, the seeker attains the kingdom.

The second way to find Shambhala is by stumbling upon it. The traveler is amazed and enchanted, but he is not enlightened enough to see the place for what it truly is. He hasn't done his own work, so he doesn't understand that the kingdom is the heart, the deepest part of the self. Or that the tasty fruits are really the fruits of Spirit: love, joy, peace, patience, kindness, goodness, faithfulness, gentleness and self-control. Nor does he realize that the precious gems and metals are really great spiritual truths, or that the freedom from illness, disease and old age are the rewards of self-realization: at-onement with God.

The accidental tourist instead takes the place on face value. For a while, he enjoys himself, but soon tires of the unrelenting goodness of it. He longs for the world he knew. He departs, confident that he can find this kingdom again whenever he wants. But once he leaves, the mists close in and Shambhala is lost. It can only be found again through the spiritual search.

The Christian parallel to Shambhala is the quest for the Holy Grail, symbolized by a cup or chalice made of precious metal and rimmed with pearls and encrusted with jewels. In the principal stories about the Grail, the knights of King

Arthur's Roundtable search through the wilderness (the unconscious) for the Grail, gaining wisdom and purifying themselves through their experiences and travails.

These and other myths are part of alchemy mystery teachings found in cultures East and West since ancient times. Elements of these stories of the quest for the essential self show up in our dreams, and remind us of our true treasures and our true blessings.

FINDING TREASURE

The following dream contains alchemical symbolism:

I was in a forest, looking for mushrooms. There weren't any, for it wasn't the season. But I kneeled on the ground and started scratching the soil with my fingers. It was a light black soil, damp and soft, forest soil. Under an inch of soil I found lots of small gold coins and small gold objects, very heavy and very shiny. They shone like the sun. I was very surprised to find gold so easily. I took the coins and little sculptures, put them in a red-and-white-checkered handkerchief and kept them in my pocket. I was very aware that this gold belonged to me.

The dreamer finds herself in the forest of the unconscious, looking for spiritual nourishment (mushrooms, or food) that isn't there. Often we look for what we want in the wrong place at the wrong time. The black forest soil represents the beginning stage of alchemy, called the *nigredo*, or blackening. The old must die before the new can be born. The black forest soil has been enriched with the decay and death of vegetation. Vegetation is a symbol of both life and death/rebirth, and thus it is a mediator between the conscious and the unconscious. The gold coins and objects that shine like the sun are the end result of alchemy, the gold of enlightenment, or as Jung described it, individuation, the process of becoming whole. The dreamer takes possession of them and knows emphatically that they are hers. Red and white in alchemy symbolize the masculine and feminine, respectively. The red-and-white-checkered handkerchief symbolizes the balance of the inner masculine and feminine that is part of the process of individuation.

This dream came at the beginning of a spiritual awakening for the dreamer, providing a road map of sorts and an advance preview of the journey ahead. Any journey has its difficulties and obstacles, and every traveler faces moments when it seems more prudent to turn back than continue. Knowing that the gold is there fuels faith to continue.

GOING INTO THE DEPTHS

Here is another dream with alchemical imagery:

M. and I are on a slim, irregular hunk of driftwood serving as a raft out in the vast ocean. I have with me a white plastic grocery bag that contains an article of clothing, some other items I do not recall, and a gold ring that is very valuable to me. No sooner do I set the bag down on the raft than it plops into the ocean and sinks. I am upset. I look into the water. It is crystal clear, and far below I see a sunken island. Many things seem to have sunk in this area. The island is so far below that I know I cannot dive into the water to search for the bag—the pressure would be too great. I wonder if I can bring some divers back. How will my little bag be found? What if the ring fell out of the bag and is gone forever?

In her journal, the dreamer recorded the following thoughts:

Immediately what comes to mind is the gold ring on the merry-go-round: reaching for the gold. Here I must go far down into the depths of the unconscious and the emotions to retrieve the gold. The gold also refers to the gold of the alchemists, and going into the depths means plumbing the inner world, the unconscious, in order to get there. I must go into my own depths—and withstand the pressure—to retrieve my own inner riches. The sunken island is my own creativity, far down in the depths. But I can see it clearly—I know where to go.

M. is the dreamer's husband. The dreamer had been working as a novelist for several years, making a comfortable living writing formula fiction. Lately she had longed to stretch herself beyond formula to more challenging writing. Such a change is not always easy when publishers and readers like a writer just as she is.

In the dream, she interpreted the driftwood raft as her present work—she was just drifting. The item of clothing represented her identity that she wished to change. The valuable gold ring was her creativity. M. is simply present in the dream. In life, he was supportive of his wife's career, willing to ride whatever ship (or raft) she chose.

The message for the dreamer was that the only way she would ever retrieve the ring—that is, expand her creativity—was to dive into the depths herself and take a risk. If she did not take the risk, then a new level of artistic expression and a new career might become what is "gone forever."

One of the greatest treasures we can discover with the help of our dreams is our true purpose in life. In the next dream, royal tools of pure gold carry a powerful message to a young woman searching for meaning:

From on high I am given a sacred blessed role and responsibility. A golden orb and scepter are lowered into my arms. I feel very humble as I watch this scene, for I am inaudibly asked by a Higher Power to carry these regal symbols of spiritual calling and mighty leadership down into the valley for the healing and well-being of humanity. I am completely awed by this message.

The dreamer's marriage was failing. She decided to go into Jungian analysis in order to understand why she was so unhappy with her husband. They had met when she was seventeen and in the first week of college. In the beginning he had been her best friend. About a year and a half after she started analysis, they separated. Divorce came two and a half years later.

The dreamer explained:

I did not know what my life path was to be. I had expected to be forever married and to live happily ever after. I had many blessings and two gorgeous little boys. So many changes were happening. I had gone back into theater training. I was now a single parent. I was on a spiritual path but had no idea where it would take me. I had no idea what work I was meant to do when my alimony ran out. I felt I had some kind of "calling" but I didn't know what it was.

The dream about the orb and scepter seemed to me to be about my highest purpose. The dream moved me profoundly. And is my favorite all-time dream because I felt I was being "gifted" with my highest purpose.

Since then I have realized the orb and scepter are very old symbols of the sacred marriage between king and country, the masculine and the feminine. The orb is to be held in the left hand, the scepter in the right. I always seem to be needing to balance the male side with the female side.

In my dream the orb and scepter were of pure gold, unadorned by jewels. The gold was the holiest and purist gold that can only come from "the grace of heaven." I received these symbols of "spiritual rulership" in complete humility, when alone, on the top of a mount overlooking the world in the valley below.

LOVE AND SELF-WORTH

Money can symbolize our own self-worth:

I was walking down the street with my best friend (someone I had never actually seen in "real" life). It was the street of a city and we were headed toward an Irish festival. . . . There were thousands of people cramming the street and the festival was supposedly for a good cause. We were to hear the plight of some homeless Irish folks and hear how badly things were for them in this country. My friend and I were standing near the stage and I threw a dollar onto it because I wanted to help a good cause. I threw it before any of the Irish people were even onstage yet.

A person came onstage who was very small—the body of a small child—skinny little legs. But, the face of a grown-up man—dark, curly hair, beard and mustache. He was wearing a loose one-piece suit that was white with green clovers all over it. People were throw-

ing money onto the stage. And there were gypsies out among the crowds collecting money.

I was angry because I knew the little performer was not home-less—it was obvious this was just a total sham performance. In ret-rospect the little man reminded me of a leprechaun. Anyway, the head gypsy came up to the front of the crowd and was handing out money to the other gypsies and the little performer. They had col-lected massive amounts of money. I thought it was obscene they had collected so much for something that was obviously a complete sham. And I also thought it was obscene that the gypsies were di-viding up their take in front of the crowd. Couldn't anyone see this was false? Didn't anyone care?

This dream dealt with self-worth issues for the dreamer. The dream best friend was her Higher Self. In mythology, such figures are often magical traveling companions who aid the traveler—they are symbolic of one's intuition and un-tapped powers.

Subconsciously, the dreamer felt she did not deserve the approval and respect of others, symbolized by the throwing of money. Like the leprechaun, she felt she was not really what others thought she was. Though she tried to think well of herself, she was not generous in her self-appraisal, sym-bolized by the desire to help but the contribution of only one dollar. The best friend, her intuition, is passive in the dream: present but not called upon to participate.

The dreamer was undergoing some serious health and financial challenges. Others in her life were sympathetic, supportive and helpful. The dream revealed her difficulty accepting this genuine outpouring of concern. Didn't others know she was really a sham? The dream served as a mech-anism for a change in awareness.

ROSEMARY ELLEN GUILEY

Sometimes dreams provide a tonic we need. The following dream occurred to a thirty-seven-year-old woman and literally changed her life:

I was going through a particularly rough time. I was grieving my father's death, my marriage was in trouble and I was suffering severe panic and anxiety attacks that led to a deep depression. I had difficulty sleeping and had nightmarish dreams when I could sleep. All this occurred toward the end of a very cold and dark winter and I began wondering if I was losing my sanity.

I reached a point one night where I just gave in . . . I wanted to experience joy again so badly that I thought: OK, if this is how my life is going to be then I will be happy right here, right now, instead of waiting until I "feel better," which might never happen. I went to bed feeling that resolve and also believing that I could withstand the worst that my "dark side" could throw at me while sleeping. As I fell asleep, I heard several musical voices calling my name . . . and I felt a sensation of floating in complete comfort. I saw a beautiful star field . . . and then a strand of stars separated from the rest, coming toward me. I felt many hands place this beautiful necklace around my neck in a gesture of blessing. I felt a profound sense of love, encouragement and acceptance. I slept well through the night and had the best rest I'd had for many weeks. The depression was gone the next morning and with it the fear and anticipation of panic/ anxiety attacks: I have not had one since that night. Everything in my life did not become "perfect" overnight, but I have regained my self-esteem, and a sense of real security and peace. I often think about that dream . . . and feel certain that I am loved and cherished by the Creator of that necklace. I know I am wearing it even now . . . a billion carats worth of stars.

Since that dream, I pay attention to whatever my subconscious (or superconscious) has to say. I love the subtle language of symbols and layers of meanings, and consider my dreams to be a very important part of my spiritual life.

In summary, to get the most out of dreams about money, valuables and treasure, always look for a spiritual component. A dream may primarily address a monetary situation in life, but it also is likely to contain important insights into the real treasure of the Self.

EIGHT

Other People

Other people play important roles in our dream dramas. Many of them we know—they are family members, friends, coworkers, casual acquaintances. Sometimes they are strangers, but remind us of someone we know—they are and aren't that person. And sometimes they are complete strangers to us.

Everyone in a dream tells us something about ourselves. Dreams make use of our relationships and interactions with others to reveal our emotions, attitudes and opportunities for change. For example, if you have a hostile relationship with someone, a dream involving that person might be asking you to examine your emotions about, and emotional responses to, certain situations or circumstances.

Sometimes other people mirror qualities, attitudes and

behavior in us. In analyzing dream figures, ask yourself how
they remind you of yourself. Sometimes other people represent a quality we find lacking in ourselves and would like to develop. For example, you dream of a casual acquaintance, and in dreamwork associate him with risk-taking and confidence. Perhaps you wish to be more confident in general—or you are in a situation that calls for confident risk-taking.

Children

Children in dreams can represent ourselves at the same age, or reflect a time period related to their age, such as four years ago, four months ago, four weeks ago, four days ago. They can also represent emotional or behavioral patterns that might be present in your life at the time of the dream. Infants and newborns often are symbols for something new being birthed in life.

I was in a crowd and suddenly came upon a lost child, a little girl about four or five years old. I took her home and was so very glad that I had enough to support her. I adopted her. She learned to love me and we lived very happily together. It seems I was in business, doing very well at it, and evenings came home to her exclusively—just we two. I seemed to think that that was all I needed—an outlet for love and to receive love in return.[1]

The child looked like the dreamer at the same age, when she had felt unloved at home. In the dream, she is able to love, support and nurture herself, and to give and receive love freely.

Our parents in dreams can reflect us as parents or represent qualities of being a father or mother. Often dream parents really do concern our real parents—we are always their child, and they have shaped our life.

I'm at a theater watching a mother and daughter perform a play. The girl is obviously uneasy and doesn't know her lines. Every time she starts to speak there's some disturbance or distraction and she shuts up. Finally the mother speaks her lines for her.

In this dream, the dreamer, a woman, is both mother and daughter. The mother also represents her own mother as well. When she was growing up, her mother embarrassed her with the thoughtless behavior of correcting her in public and finishing her sentences for her. This undermined the girl's confidence, and as she grew older she was often unsure of herself. The dream scenario reenacted these earlier events in a symbolic way. The dream mother also represented the dreamer's own inner mother, a scolding inner voice that was inhibiting.

Authority Figures

Authority figures, such as police officers, judges, teachers, doctors and so on, represent the disciplinarian within us. In dreams, they take remedial action when we have overstepped our bounds, are going off in the wrong direction, or need to slow down. Here is one of my dreams:

I am driving a little white sports car that is shaped like an ovoid, very futuristic. It is barely big enough to hold me. I am driving through city streets. The car wants to go very fast. I look in my rearview mirror and see that I am being followed by a police car. It is a large white ovoid, unmarked, but I can see the radar gun inside. I know I am speeding and slow down. The policeman does not pull me over, but keeps following me. It's easy to drive the car fast, though, and I have a hard time slowing down. As I turn a corner, the car speeds up. The officer turns on his flashing lights and pulls me over. He comes up to the window, and I know he is going to write me a ticket. I start to offer an excuse, and then decide not to, as I am sure he always hears excuses. But I do tell him, "You were just following me, waiting to catch me speeding." Then I start to cry. I try not to, because I think he probably always sees women cry in an attempt to get out of a ticket. I have a hard time holding back the tears. There are people in the street watching.

I was literally speeding through life—so busy that I could barely manage everything I was attempting to do—symbolized by the car that is barely big enough to hold me. It is futuristic because I am pursuing plans to build my future. All of these activities, however, had taken control of me. The dream car speeds along on its own and is hard to control and slow down. Even when I know I am being watched by the police—I know I should slow down in waking life—I keep motoring along. Finally everything catches up with me and the policeman stops me. The ticket is a symbol to ease up. "I have to slow down," I thought. "I am not entirely in control. I am stressed. Now I must pay the consequences, in front of everybody, just like in the dream, where others watch me go through the embarrassment of getting a ticket."

Other authority figures are doctors and nurses, who often relate to healing issues. Teachers, guides and "wise elders" in dreams often portray the Higher Self wisdom we acquire through life experience. This wisdom sees the big picture and speaks to us through the intuition.

I was with some man who seemed like a wise teacher. He helped me on with my coat and asked if I'd like to drive a car. I said I couldn't. He said: "I'll teach you." After I'd gone I wondered why I had been so foolish as to say I couldn't drive when actually I can. Now I think of it, there was a sort of "vision" dream which preceded. It seemed that I was looking down a long passage which had a light at the end. This light would come and go and I was happy when I saw it come. I thought of it as a star of hope.[2]

The dreamer was a man who had wandered from one job to another in different fields. Prior to this dream, he had settled for an outdoor occupation that was pleasant but not taxing, and did not call upon his creative abilities. He intuitively felt that he would "see the light" about life. The dream validates this, as the star of hope, though it is not always in view.

The wise teacher is a symbol for the dreamer's Higher Self, showing him that he can do what he apparently thinks he cannot, or else does not want to do. He knows he can drive his car, or his life, but demurs. "It strikes me that a lot of my trouble has been the habit of saying 'no' to life and saying 'no' to myself," he said. Part of him was pushing himself forward and part of him was holding himself back.

It's not unusual to dream of people we know. They, too, often symbolize something we see or desire in ourselves. Many dreamers are puzzled why acquaintances, whom they do not know well, or people they have not seen for a long time, suddenly become major actors in a dream drama. Besides symbolizing characteristics, attitudes or behaviors, these dream figures may evoke an emotional response within us that is the clue to understanding the meaning of a dream. One way to work with such dreams is to make an emotional connection with the past. There may be a similar situation in the present that is evoking the same emotions. Such was the case with the next dream:

I'm getting off a boat with K. (ex-husband) and to my right I see B. Christianson (a former lover) with a baby in a stroller. The baby looks exactly like him. I'm not sure if B. is a man or a woman so I don't recognize him at first. We walk to his house. I want to tell him why I never called him back and need to wait until K. is not around. The baby was placed in lukewarm water by a grandmotherly figure to clean off doo-doo. I thought the water was too cold for the baby and was worried about the baby. The house was in disrepair, pillars needed painting. I went to another room and B.'s wife was there with another woman. In the corner of the room there was a setup like a beauty parlor and his wife was giving her friend a consultation about makeup. Later I had a chance to walk alone with B. and I told him why I had not called. K. was jealous and I did not want any hassles. Also I was unhappy and was afraid I'd want to have an affair. I told him I was leaving K. as soon as I made sure I was financially secure.

The people in this dream were long out of the dreamer's life when she had the dream. Puzzling over why she was dreaming about people she hadn't seen in years, the dreamer then realized that they were symbols of states of her own consciousness and emotions—all of which she could relate to events in her present life.

The dream ends with her concerns over financial security. At the time of the dream, she was launching her own business and was indeed concerned about financial security. This new direction is symbolized by the baby, whose excrement symbolized to the dreamer that "It's not comfortable going through all this shit." But wisdom and experience—symbolized by the grandmotherly figure—take care of things. The dreamer's concern for the baby reflects her concern that the conditions (symbolized by the water temperature) are right for getting the business off to a good start.

The surname Christianson relates to the dreamer's spiritual studies. The baby who looks just like Christianson symbolized to the dreamer that "We reflect the image of Christ." The dreamer does not recognize him at first—or even know if he is a man or woman. This meant to her that "We don't see the God in us." Walking to Christianson's house symbolized "our path in life is to go home again" in a spiritual sense. "I lost touch with my Higher Self when I was married to K.," said the dreamer, "and walking alone with B. meant getting back in touch with myself."

Strangers in dreams represent something within us as well. Perhaps it is something we have not yet acknowledged within us, or a part of us that troubles us. Or, they are messengers of our Higher Self, bringing intuitive guidance to our attention.

There were some old men fussing around a place like the board-room of our organization and they seemed somehow hostile. Then I was aware of a spiral which rose through the ceiling and widened as it rose. A Mr. _____ was present and there seemed to be some understanding between him and me as I climbed along the mantelpiece to reach the spiral. Then it seemed as if I must immediately get at the job of packing up so as to catch a train which was going a long way and which I mustn't miss.[3]

The dreamer considered himself an innovative, forward thinker who, in his work, had to contend with people he considered to be narrow-minded, fussy about details and locked into procedures. Mr. _____ was a likeable, respected member of the organization—a role model for the dreamer. In the dream, they share a rapport and a common understanding that they are on the same wavelength. The spiral to the ceiling represents an ascent to a higher level of thinking or consciousness. The old men are not just other people whom the dreamer views as obstacles, but that part of himself that fusses about change and resists the innovative, forward-thinking part of himself. The dream is urging the dreamer to go beyond his own bounds and not be limited by other people. He has a long way to go—if he catches the train out of limitations.

Here is another example of a stranger in a dream:

I met a young woman in her apartment. She was a psychic, or rather a messenger from above. She wore a large pink dress. She made me sit down and immediately said: "You're waiting to hear from someone." I said yes. She said: "You're not hearing from him, and you won't for a long time." She looked really sorry about this. I felt terrible. But then she said: "But it will happen. It will come true. Eventually you will be together," and she looked much happier. I said "Thank you!" and she said: "Don't thank me, it's a great honor for me to take care of you."

The dreamer interpreted the psychic young woman as her own Higher Self—literally the "messenger from above." Pink is a color associated with love, and the young woman had a loving energy about her. The message involved the dreamer's anxiety over a romantic relationship. She was afraid the man had lost interest in her. The dreamer was greatly reassured by the dream. Indeed, we are always taken care of by the Higher Self.

In the next dream, a woman is portrayed by an insane woman, whom she tries to control with love, but is imprisoned by her:

I was working as a domestic in some home where there was an insane woman. I thought I could conquer this woman by loving her. I looked at her very closely and lovingly and thought she was responding to it. She put her arms around me and seized me tightly, loving me but clinging, and I was at a loss how to get free from her.[4]

The dreamer was undergoing a great deal of psychological stress and was afraid of going insane. Her thoughts about her dream were:

The insane woman for some reason makes me think of myself when in my teens. I also am reminded of one of my types of dream in which I am on a witness stand saying that I'm not guilty. This brings up mother in childhood. Thinking I could win the woman by love is like an idea, or rather a firm belief, I've had that loving people will bring out the best in them. . . .

The woman seizing me seems to make things complicated. I think of it first as a part of myself holding on to and holding down another part of me so that it can't escape and get out. And yet both myself and the woman were loving; only the woman seemed to show her love at a lower level. But if she and I are identified, it would be me loving myself but bringing about my downfall by holding back my growth.[5]

The same dreamer had another dream that revealed her inner conflict with accepting herself:

Someone told me how to do something with a tennis racquet and ball. No memory of any nets. It was a place where the ground sloped. Somehow the ball got down that hill but someone returned it. Then as I got ready to do some especially fine thing with the ball, the girls crowded around so closely that I didn't have room to swing the racquet. This irritated me greatly. The next thing I remember is feeling great hate toward a girl and saying to her, "You didn't make your brains, did you?" It seems she had been boasting about her mentality. I hated her so I wished to hit her, and it almost seemed as if I did, with the tennis racquet.[6]

The dream reminded the dreamer of an old desire to "amount to something" like other girls she'd known. She had been particularly jealous of a girl who was beautiful and clever at whatever she chose to do. But the dreamer also recognized that her struggle against the group of girls, as well as her hatred toward the one girl, represented her inner struggle and "a hate against part of myself." She felt that part of herself held her back while part of herself wished to succeed.

Every person in a dream has something to tell you about yourself. Conduct a dialogue with that dream figure and ask what its purpose and message are. Start with the persons with whom you feel the most resonance and energy, but don't overlook others. Sometimes minor players in dreams carry the messages of greatest import.

NINE

Celebrities and Famous People from History and Literature

We often dream of being with famous people in friendly, familiar and even intimate settings. But we often feel silly admitting such dreams to others—such scenarios truly seem beyond our "wildest dreams" of waking life. Shopping with a celebrity, dining with a head of state, falling in love with a rock star all are perfectly normal in the dreamworld, however.

Just like ordinary people in dreams, celebrities and famous people represent a piece of us or potential—something we admire and would like to see in ourselves. Whatever we admire about a high-profile person—clothing, behavior, intelligence, talent—is symbolized by them in dreams. Their celebrity status adds to the importance of the dream message. In waking life, we take notice of what famous people do. Dream celebrities ask us to pay special attention.

Stars

The following dream involves a rock star, Jim Morrison, the late lead singer of The Doors, who was idolized by a woman during her college years. She was long since past his music, and was surprised when he appeared in a realistic dream:

I am going to school at some college. I walk by a tavern and see, to my surprise, Jim Morrison singing there. He looks just the same as he did more than twenty years ago when I was in college as a kid. A woman friend of mine (no one I know in waking life) is waiting outside for him. I discover she is a good friend of his. I tell her I want to meet him.

When he comes out, I go up to him and ask for his autograph. I feel silly, but I really want it. I have a small notepad with me. He signs it. He is so handsome. He hasn't changed a bit in all those years. I think I could fall in love with him. I decide that I will go to see him sing at the tavern often.

All I can think about is Jim Morrison. I wonder why he has never done anything else in his life. Why is he still singing the same old songs, as great as they are? Why didn't he go to college? Then I realize that he is doing what he does best.

This dream is very real and pleasurable. I am happy in it, and infatuated with Jim.

Then I wake up to go to the bathroom. I sort of carry the dream along with me. I think how great it is to meet Jim Morrison. Then suddenly I realize—wait a minute, he's dead! I can't have met him— it's only a dream.

The dreamer was her own age in the dream. Though Morrison had been singing for twenty years in the dream, he still looked youthful. The dreamer was going through the ups and downs of midlife, when many people make an assessment of what they have done—and haven't done. She had been wondering if she had made right decisions concerning her career, and often thought how life might have been different (or perhaps better) had she followed other paths.

The life of Jim Morrison symbolizes quite a polarity of characteristics. He was creative, a free spirit and wild. His indulgences in alcohol and drugs killed him.

For the dreamer, Morrison's creative and free spirit were the characteristics that spoke to her. As a musician, he did what he wanted to do, and what he did best. She realized that she had done that, too, in making her choices. Doors are symbols of opportunities, and the dreamer found a connection to "The Doors" and her choices.

People in midlife feel the pressure of time. Suddenly life appears to be half over, and goals remain unaccomplished. The dreamer was feeling this pressure to make the most of her time. Morrison lost his talent and his life to substance abuse. The dreamer was not a substance abuser, but felt this symbolized wasting talent and time through distractions. The dream was telling her to stay focused and not allow distractions to "kill" her creativity.

In the dream, she feels she can easily fall in love with Morrison. In her dreamwork, she asked herself what characteristics or qualities she wanted to love, or bring out in herself. Her answer was "do what you really want to do, not what you think you should do, or what will get the approval of others."

In the next dream, the dreamer finds herself on friendly terms with an actor:

I am at a conference and seem to be part of the staff. There is a big room with a long table in it. A planning room. I go in periodically and find celebrities there just sitting at the table. I think, "Management has brought in celebrities for us." It's as though they are there to entertain the staff. I walk in once and find Louis Jourdan sitting at the table. No one is talking to him. I think, "Wow, the vampire!" and almost blurt it out. I stop myself, thinking he has done many film roles and may not appreciate being remembered as the vampire. Instead I say, "Hello, Louis!" He says hello back. Then I think that I have been very impertinent to call him by his first name, when he doesn't know me, and I know who he is, but I don't really know him. I resolve to apologize later. I think no one talks to these celebrities because they're shy or afraid to.

The dreamer acknowledged that when Louis Jourdan was at the peak of his popularity, she found him to be attractive and sexy, and especially liked his seductive portrayal of Dracula. In the dream, she is the only person who recognizes the actor; others ignore him altogether.

She related these factors to herself: she was an artist of some accomplishment, but had not achieved the recognition she desired. She often felt that her work "just sat there" unappreciated.

She noted that the Jourdan dream figure did not seem to be particularly upset at not being noticed by many people. She felt the dream was giving her a message about knowing her own worth and not being shy about it.

Celebrities show up anywhere in dreams—even in bathrooms. Bathrooms are places of our greatest intimacy—bodily functions—and our greatest vulnerability and need for privacy. We may willingly bare all in the bedroom, but we expect privacy in the bathroom. We would be upset if someone famous walked in on us in the bathroom, but in dreams, anything can happen:

I'm in the bathroom of my house, fixing my hair and makeup. There are clothes of mine hanging in the room, like you find in a closet. Other people are in the house. Suddenly the door opens and Jimmy Stewart comes in. When he sees me, he is hesitant, but I say, "It's okay, come on in."

The dreamer felt this dream related to personal changes that concerned her sense of self-comfort, empowerment and outward appearances. She did free association with the actor Jimmy Stewart, describing him as a "sensitive male." The welcoming of him into her place of greatest privacy represented an awakening—and welcoming—of a masculine energy and expression into her life. She was learning to become more authoritative and powerful, but in a tempered way that was influenced by her nurturing feminine side. The clothes represented her new outward appearances waiting to be worn. This was further reinforced in the dream by her paying attention to her hair and makeup. The dream was telling her that her inner changes were manifesting in new outward behavior that was noticeable to others. She was comfortable with, and desirous of, these changes.

In the next example, a dreamer is romantic with an actor:

I was on a chairlift (ski area) with Mel Gibson—a male I adored. The chairlift was actually going up the center of a department store and we were riding above the elevators and could see each floor and all its activities and wares off to each side. As we reached each new level in the store, Mel was horsing around with staff and store customers. He stayed so long on one floor that he got left behind and I was still riding the chair. He dropped whatever he was doing and ran up some stairs, or took the elevator to catch up with me at each level. As I slowly "crested the hill," or climbed to a new level in the store, Mel would spring out of the elevator holding a big bouquet of flowers. Or, he would be standing off to the side in the store holding a big, goofy, inflatable toy. Everything he did I felt was very romantic and he was so silly that he made me really laugh. When I realized I was still on the chairlift and still moving forward and he wasn't with me, he did everything he could—put on all his charm—to get my attention at every level. And, as is Mel Gibson in real life, he was very distracting and the center of my focus.

In her journal, the dreamer noted, "The more I write the more I realize this obviously has something to do with my feminine 'climbing higher' but I am distracted by the very appealing masculine at every level." The dreamer was coping with health and financial challenges and was immersed in spiritual study for support. The department store represented choices, and the chairlift and elevator represented a rising of consciousness. The flowers, fun, charm and laughter were elements she needed more of in her life.

Powerful People

Famous people in dreams carry weight as authority figures. The following dream might have far less impact if the dreamer were chatting with a friend:

The president of the United States and I were sitting with our backs against a grass-covered bank. We were quite close together. He looked at me in a warmly friendly manner, smiling and understanding.[1]

Authority figures such as the president of the United States can be symbols for father or mother. The dreamer related this dream to her father, and her desire for him to understand her better. This matter was very important to her, also symbolized by the office of the presidency.

Religious Figures

We are impressed by celebrities and heads of state, but the top of the list of Most Important People belongs to religious figures, such as saints, sages, prophets, biblical figures, Mother Mary, and Jesus:

I dreamed I was the private secretary to our Lord Jesus Christ. Anyone who wished to see Him had to consult me first. The president of the corporation for which I had been working appeared, and asked to see the Lord. I told him I was sorry, but I could not disturb the Lord now, and he would have to come some other time.[2]

The dreamer had been laid off work about two weeks prior to having the dream. The dreamer had suffered a loss of self-esteem, and regains it in the dream by having a supremely important position. Now he was much more important than the company president.

Theatrical critic and playwright William Archer had this dream about Christ:

An odd dream of which I remember very little, to this effect: I was somehow or other a relation—a brother, I think—of Christ. I expected his second coming, not on theological grounds, but rather as a piece of family news, and thought it my duty to prepare for it. So I found myself in a railway station haranguing the bookstall clerk on faith—making a formal, oratorical speech, though I have no recollection of any audience except the clerk. I said that faith was the great thing—it did not matter what you believed, as long as you believed something. *I had an impression of being very unctuous and eloquent, but the clerk was obdurate and quite unimpressed.*

I myself was not at all in an emotional condition. It seemed quite a matter of course. Nor did I think of Christ's second advent as a catastrophic, world-shaking event. I seemed rather to expect him to arrive by the next train. I can trace absolutely *no connection with any waking experience or thought.*[3]

This dream occurred shortly after the death of Archer's only child, Tom, in World War I. Archer grieved deeply and turned to Spiritualism. Christ, who was resurrected from the dead, is a symbol for the desire for the return, or resurrection, of his son—a family event. Many grieving relatives turned to Spiritualism in World War I, and Archer, as a respected literary man and intellectual, may have been criticized by some of his peers for his interests. Thus he lectures the bookstall (newsstand) clerk on the importance of having faith in whatever you believed. Perhaps some of his critics were as unswayed as the clerk in the dream.

In the aftermath shock of the death of a loved one, we often expect them to return at any minute and erase the horrible mistake that's been made about their demise. In the dream, Archer expects the resurrected Christ, a symbol for his son, to be on the next train.

Mother Mary is the key figure in the next dream:

I was at a house where people were eating cherry pie and they invited me to have some. There was something said about how the boys were busy tinkering with electricity and making a statue of the Madonna.[4]

A great deal was revealed in this short dream of a school-teacher who felt unfulfilled by both her marriage and job. Eating cherry pie is sensual, and electricity is often a symbol for sexual energy. Both symbols can be interpreted as relating to pent-up sexual energy. The Madonna, or Virgin Mary, represents someone who is above sensuality and sexuality. A statue is inert. The dreamer was unmarried and had no romantic relationship.

The Madonna reminded the dreamer of a pageant called "The Miracle." According to the story line, a nun falls in love with a knight, who rescues her from the nunnery and takes her out into the real world. The knight is killed and then the nun is beset by a series of men, including a robber and an insane emperor. The dreamer acknowledged that throughout her life she had entertained a fantasy of "the person whose love would unlock every door for me and make life a completely fulfilling experience." The shadow side of this fantasy, however, is the potential for a downfall of honor, as symbolized by the nun in the story. The dreamer associated the Madonna with sympathy and understanding—two qualities she continually applied to her acceptance of her less-than-ideal life.

Famous Characters

Besides famous people, we also dream about famous characters from books, plays and stories. William Shakespeare's doomed lovers, Romeo and Juliet, have become symbolic of love that is willing to be sacrificed in death. In this dream, Shakespeare's plot takes a different turn, becoming mixed with the fairy tale of Sleeping Beauty:

I dream of Romeo and Juliet. Romeo is lying on the stage floor as though dead. Juliet is waking up beside him. She looks like [actress] Gwyneth Paltrow and is dressed in a long golden taffeta dress, exquisitely lovely. She looks like an enchanted Princess of the Sun. Juliet is blond, gorgeous, stunning, in full bloom, health, aliveness and well-being.

She sees Romeo lying beside her, and rather than deciding to kill herself because he is dead, she makes a different choice on behalf of her new life: confidence, beauty, empowerment and well-being. She decides to live fully, wholeheartedly and vividly. Next she decides Romeo is not actually dead, just asleep, and that she will gently bring him to passionate life again by kissing him awake, just as the Prince did for Sleeping Beauty in the tale.

Juliet kisses Romeo with great love and gentleness, and Romeo starts to stir with life. He is alive and will wake up to be with her in all wholehearted fullness of being.

This dream occurred after divorce from an unhappy marriage, and represented the conscious decision of the dreamer to be alive, happy and passionate. The revival of Romeo symbolizes the renewal of her own self-love and worth, and also her knowledge that romance and passion will be part of her life again. The colors of the sun, reinforced in the blond hair and golden taffeta gown, symbolize spiritual renewal of a great magnitude. The dreamer realizes her own enlightenment. She is self-realized, independent.

The dreamer recorded these thoughts about her dream:

The dream of Romeo and Juliet I just loved. I loved it that Juliet was so beautiful, empowered, gracious, intelligent, perceptive, warm, positive and happy. She was full of light, life, and warmth in the dream.

This dream was in contrast of old dreams of the "Inner Feminine" back when I was married. I remember one dream in particular with an anemic-looking woman in a pale anemic green chiffon dress on a gurney defenseless against a horrible man trying to light her on fire with a huge torch. The dream was terrifying. Outside the door in a hall was my [then] husband totally ignorant of what was going on in the closed room. He was unconscious and uncaring of the emergency. Not only that, he was dressed in women's curlers, and had no direction to his movements and energy.

So this beautiful dream of Juliet in full color and light, dressed in a long, gorgeous, taffeta dress the color of the sun was so validating.

And the Romeo and Juliet story was going differently than in Shakespeare's version. My lovers did not have to die. Juliet had awakened. She was convinced Romeo was not dead. She was going to gently awaken and arouse Romeo with a kiss.

He was there for her. He was not going away. He had put himself asleep because he thought she was dead, or asleep, but he was there with her, her committed partner. They belonged together. In no way did he belong with anyone else except Juliet.

Juliet was queen. She knew what to do. She was very happy, and she would use love, grace, charm and insight to bring the love in her heart outward into the world. She was as warm as the morning dawn and as healthy as any Divine Feminine creature could be.

The dream seemed symbolic of the Feminine and its new liberation, freedom and empowerment on the planet. Now the Feminine has recovered, the true Masculine can awaken!

I was thrilled, charmed, delighted and encouraged by this dream.

In dreamwork, look at celebrities and famous people as symbols of characteristics, behavior and status. The presence of someone important lends the dream an extra importance, too.

TEN

The Animal Within

At first it was an unsettling dream:

I am in my house. I go to open the front door to go outside. When I open the door, I am shocked to see a large black snake coiled in front of me, looking at me. I have the feeling it is waiting for me or wants to come inside. I slam the door. I try to go out the back door, but when I open it I find the snake is there, too. I become frightened—maybe this snake will try to get in the house through the windows. I run around closing any open windows. Suddenly the snake is inside the house—I feel it. I find it coiled up on the living room sofa. At first I want to scream, but then I realize that the snake is not threatening me. It seems determined to stay. I am very wary of it.

The dreamer, a forty-two-year-old woman, awakened from this dream feeling anxious. She had a fear of snakes and wondered what this dream could possibly signify.

Snakes are powerful symbols of transformation. Because they live in the ground, they are masters of the depths, the inner wisdom. Because they shed their skin, the ancients believed them to have the power to heal themselves and to live forever. They are associated with the phallus, sex and fertilization. As "serpent power" they represent the life force within.

The dreamer of the preceding dream arrived at this interpretation:

I realized that my fear of snakes meant that the dream was bringing something to my attention that I was afraid of, or afraid to acknowledge. I saw the black snake as a symbol of something fearful in my own underworld. It wants to come into my house, that is, come fully into my life. It is ready to move in—it shows up on my doorstep and won't go away. I can't keep it out—it comes in anyway and makes itself right at home.

At the time, this woman was undergoing a major change in life. She had recently become divorced, a change initiated by her husband and not wanted by her. She was facing redefining herself. All the "old" rules no longer applied. She felt victimized and also doubted her sexual attractiveness. Understandably, this was a frightening transition—but one that had to be made. The dream helped her to realize that something new was waiting to be born. She needed to reach into her own depths, and welcome change and growth into her life.

The dreamer did active imagination with this dream, in

which she and the snake became friends. "I felt I opened the door to my own inner power," she said. The dream no longer frightened her, but became a source of encouragement.

A snake dream with similar imagery had a different meaning for a seventeen-year-old girl:

I was walking in the woods, all alone. Suddenly a terrible snake appeared on the path, and started directly at me. I can't remember exactly what happened just after this. But I was terribly frightened.

The next thing I remember was sitting down in a lovely meadow, with flowers all around. The snake was there, and I was not afraid of it anymore. I leaned back, against a tree, and sprawled out comfortably, watching the snake. It came gliding over the grass to me, and laid its head in my lap. And I was not afraid anymore. I woke up before anything happened.[1]

Here the snake has a sexual symbolism, and also that of forbidden fruit. The girl was awakening sexually but had fear about sexual encounters. Woods and forests often are symbols of the unconscious. Here she is all alone, finding her path to awakening, when suddenly a snake appears and arouses instinctual fear. She next encounters it in a more pleasing and nonthreatening situation, a meadow with beautiful flowers and a tree, a symbol of inner strength. She discovers there is nothing to fear.

Animals Are Uncensored

Human beings have always had a deep relationship with the animal realm. We have dreamed and visioned about animals since our earliest recorded history. We have seen great mystery and magic in animals. The frequency of their appearance as symbols in our religions, mythologies, art, and fairy tales indicates the intimate connection between the human soul and the animal soul. In the realm of the supernatural, animals often come to our aid. Thus it is no surprise that in our dreams animals are our greatest teachers, leading us to the threshold of awakening and transformation.

Animals are creatures of instinct. They live in their own world according to their own rules. They are neither good nor bad. They follow their instincts, and cannot do anything that is contrary to their own nature. Thus, they are always true to themselves. That is the truth they show us in dreams: how we can stay true to ourselves.

Since ancient times, human beings have seen their own instinctual natures portrayed by animals. We have used animal terms to describe traits we like and dislike in ourselves. We are "piggy" when we are greedy. We "outfox" opponents. We can "eat like a horse." We can "sing like a bird."

Dream animals have something to tell us about our instinctual, unconscious side. Quite often they represent something within us that is seeking to be integrated into the light of consciousness. This is represented in the common dream motif of being in a house in the woods with animals outside. The house is where you live, not only physically but in terms of your consciousness. The house serves as protection against the unconscious. The woods, often dark and scary, represent the unconscious. The animals represent things within the unconscious seeking to come inside—just as the snake wanted to come in to the "inner home" of the dreamer.

In the following dream, rats invade a woman's bed:

I am in bed and feel something move at my legs, around my thighs. I realize it is rats and I start to panic, then move and drive them down and out. It is like they are also inside my legs and I am squeezing them out of my body too. Then it continues, as there are more. I am now "squeezing" them out of the bottom of the covers. They are being forced through the fabric of the blanket. There must be five or six. By the end my hands are a bit messy from squeezing them out, which feels a bit repulsive.

The dreamer knew immediately what the rats represented: issues related to a negative mother complex she had been dealing with in therapy. Rats are almost universally feared, and they are renowned for their destructive gnawing. The dream spoke to inner fears "gnawing" at the dreamer that well up in such numbers that she is nearly overwhelmed. The bed is a symbol of our most intimate, innermost being.

The dreamer commented:

I awake from this dream (middle of the night) and realize this is a very significant dream, related to the negative mother complex. Just last evening I had listened to a segment on National Public Radio's "Week-end Edition." I recall at the time the story had caught my attention and I had even turned up the volume (great metaphor!) so as not to miss anything. The segment was about a woman who "stayed a child" in exchange for her mother never abandoning her. They had a totally symbiotic and enmeshed relationship and the daughter never became a fully functioning adult.

At the time I thought it was an exaggerated/magnified, extreme representation of a facet of my mother and my relationship. Her shadow side wanted/needed me to stay a child. Then that night I had this dream and awoke and realized I was squeezing out the negative mother complex. Another significant link between the story on the radio and my dream is that the radio mother and daughter even slept in the same bed together, and the dream rats were in my bed.

Thus the dream carried a positive message: the dreamer was getting rid of the rats, literally squeezing them out of her body and bed, indicating a healing process. The dream used the day residue of the radio show to convey its message.

A final interesting aspect to this dream was that it also drew upon rat imagery that arose in the dreamer eleven years earlier in sand-play therapy. "I had peeled off many layers around my relationship with my mother, including some past life ones," said the dreamer. "Basically my mother is a 'Leave It to Beaver mom' on the surface and out of an Alfred Hitchcock movie subconsciously." The rat image had lain dormant until reactivated by the dream, which gave it new power.

Then I also recalled a sand-play image I did with a large sand mound in the middle. A large rat was burrowing into the back of the mound . . . the hidden side. The front visible side of the mound had sweet innocent images. At the time the rat had symbolized to me the hidden undercurrent of the negative mother complex. Now in a dream over eleven years later I pick up this sand-play image of the rat again and now am actively forcing it out of my body and my bed. Without the previous experience of the sand play, I may not have understood the dream's meaning so easily.

Dreams of being pursued by animals—especially angry or raging animals—also indicate that something is pressing for integration. The more threatening the animal, the greater the importance to pay attention.

I'm being chased by an angry lion down the street in the town where I live. I wonder how it got out. Nobody comes to help me— in fact, no one seems to notice that I'm in danger. At one point I try to reason with the lion and be friendly with it, but when it gets close, it bites me on the arm.

The lion is a symbol of strength, courage and valor, and has been popular throughout history on coats of arms. It also represents royalty and regal bearing, and is a symbol of monarchies.

The dreamer, a man, is being pushed to exhibit more leonine qualities in life: to be stronger, bolder and even more showy about who he is. The male lion reigns as king of the beasts. But the dreamer was hiding his own glory, afraid that if he shone in any way, he would be beaten down by others or exposed as a "fraud." The dream is giving him a strong message that the old behavior is no longer appropriate, and it is time to change. The very qualities he needs chase him down his own street, and finally bite him in an effort to infuse them into his being. The arm is one of our first defenses in battle; the bite infuses leonine energy into it. We also use our arms to move things and obstacles out of our way.

With this dream, the dreamer realized he needed to be

bolder about his career. He was working in a low-profile but "safe" job that involved low risk and virtually no chance for advancement. He realized that his Higher Self was showing him the need to take risks and be challenged. The image of the lion was positive reinforcement that he had the necessary qualities to be successful.

I was at my girlfriend's house, and just as I walked into the living room, I saw a spider make a web from the ceiling to the floor. Quickly the spider wound its web around my own cat, which somehow seemed to be there, sleeping on the floor. The spider began to pull the cat toward the ceiling.

Thinking I was helping the cat, I took a broom and threw it down. As I did so, the cat sprang on me, and tried to claw out my eyes. It did not scratch my face, because I held its throat; but it did scratch my arms very badly.

As the spider was drawing the cat up to the ceiling, the cat had a smile on its face, it seemed to me, as if it liked it.[2]

The dreamer described the spider as yellow and black. A young woman in college, she associated it with a young man from Princeton University (whose colors are orange and black) whom she had met at the house of her girl friend. Spiders are crafty and spin webs to catch their prey. Here in the dream, the web quickly stretches from floor to ceiling, so there is no escape. The cat represents the sexual side of the dreamer, who wishes to be passionately ensnared by the young man. Her rational side (represented by herself in the dream) tries to fight it, but her animal nature fights back and wins out—smugly.

In the following dream, the biting animal, a snake, is not

angry. In mythology, to be bitten by a snake is to be infused with a gift of wisdom from the gods—a fortunate event.

I was trying to run through a wide airport track, at night. I was desperately trying to escape from something but my feet were very heavy, I couldn't run fast, and the tarmac was rubber-like, sort of sticking to my feet. I could proceed, but slower than I wanted to. It was late at night and this airport track reminded me of the one I crossed in Africa, coming down from the airplane to meet the man who was picking me up at the airport.

While I was trying to run, I suddenly felt a terrible pain in my back—just below my left axilla. It was like a deep, burning bite and it filled my whole body with a fiery pain. Something was biting me. When I woke up, the pain was still there. It vanished as I got completely awake, so I knew it belonged to the dream only. While waking up, I had a very strong feeling of fear and anguish, which identified a nightmare to me. I had to get up, drink some water and take a few steps to find myself again in the "everyday" world. When I got back to bed I had a vision of the thing that bit my back from behind, and I clearly saw a large golden snake, flying in the air and chasing me to bite me below the shoulder. It didn't only have a golden color, it looked like it was made of gold.

The dreamer had recently returned from Africa, where she had gone on a spiritual pilgrimage. The trip had been filled with intense and transforming experiences for her, and had helped her to face the need to make some changes in her life. But once back home, it was easy to slip back into routine and status quo. In the dream, she attempts to run from change, but has a hard time getting away. The airport symbolizes the desire to escape by flight, but there is no plane in sight. The snakebite in the back seals her inability to run away. She is bitten by awareness and knowledge and has to deal with it, even if it is painful. The golden color of the snake symbolizes enlightenment and reason.

Sometimes angry, attacking animals represent other people in the dreamer's life, as in the next dream:

> *My husband and I are walking in the city at night. We come to a small park between the streets. We see a fawn lying in the park, either sleeping or resting. As we walk, we get closer to the fawn. Suddenly, the fawn jumps up and runs toward us. We see that the fawn is rabid, foaming at the mouth and bearing its teeth. My husband and I run in different directions. At first, the fawn chases my husband, but he escapes. Then the fawn turns and chases me. I am running in slow motion with the fawn getting closer and closer. When I am trapped in a stairwell I wake up with a start.*

Normally, we would think of a fawn as a sweet, gentle creature. At first glance, this fawn seems to be passive and safe, but turns rabid and dangerous. The dreamer knew just such a person:

> *I immediately realized the dream was about my husband's ex-wife. On the surface, she seems to be one of the sweetest, nicest persons in the world. Yet, over the years she has viciously attacked us over and over again, even using her children as a means of attack. At the time of the dream, she was about to take us to court, to our surprise. She lost, but I developed chronic fatigue syndrome during the stress that I experienced. Over the years, the focus of her attacks seemed to shift from my husband to me.*

Although the focus of the dream, the fawn, was another person, the dream's deep message was about the dreamer's emotional state and reaction to the stress. Unlike the dream, she was not trapped without escape.

Hidden or Camouflaged Animals

Dreams of alligators or crocodiles are common, such as this one:

> *I'm standing beside a lake, and I see that it is filled with alligators. They don't come out and bother me. I have this dream repeatedly.*

Alligators and crocodiles represent hidden dangers, or the dangers that lie below the surface (or outside of awareness). They lie just beneath the surface of the water, very little of them showing, camouflaged, and then strike suddenly. In dreams they can represent dangers of which we may be unaware. We feel safe or are not concerned, but we actually are at risk.

A body of water filled with alligators, such as in this dream, related to the dreamer's outlook on life. He was timid and always looking for reasons why something wouldn't work (and thus shouldn't be tried). There were always dangers all around him. But the dream shows that the dangers are contained: he is on land and they are in water. The dream helped him to confront unfounded fears and anxieties.

Wild animals which are forcibly contained, such as in zoos or cages, may point to repressed impulses. Wild animals that break out of their containers symbolize the consequences of repression.

In the following dream, repression takes the form of stuffed animals:

> I go down into the basement of my house and find boxes that contain stuffed animal toys. The boxes are very dusty—it's obvious that no one has looked inside of them for a long time. Some of the animals seem to be toys that I had in childhood. Others are new. I have no place to put them so I leave them in the boxes. The animals somehow come to life and come upstairs. They start tearing around and are very destructive. I think, "Holy cow!" and wonder how do I get them back in their boxes?

The dreamer, a thirty-eight-year-old man, could identify several animals: a lion, a shark, and a buffalo. He acknowledged that they represented undesirable traits within himself. He worked in a highly competitive industry. He was a cutthroat (the shark) and prided himself on it and boasted about his conquests (the lion). He liked to get his way and impose his will on others (the buffalo). He thought these personality traits were confined to work (safely stuffed into the animal toys); however, they were spilling into his personal life and affecting his relationships. Life was getting out of balance.

The dreamer felt that going into his basement symbolized his readiness to deal with these issues, though he didn't recognize it in the dream. Putting the stuffed animals back into the boxes only intensified their energy into a potentially destructive force. A breakthrough for the dreamer was his exclamation, "Holy cow!" The cow is a peaceful, docile animal and in many mythologies is a symbol for the Mother Goddess who nurtures all life. The dreamer felt that this represented his anima, or his feminine side. In order to heal himself he needed to draw upon his softer feminine qualities.

Sick or Injured Animals

Sick or injured animals often symbolize something we are neglecting about or within ourselves:

I buy more parakeets in addition to the two I already have. I capture two wild finches. Someone, like a pet-shop dealer, tells me there is something wrong with the birds and they will not survive. I put them in a cage with a little food and place them in a closet to let them die.

Later, perhaps weeks, I go to the closet and see the result of my cruelty. All the birds are still alive, to my surprise, but are suffering terribly. I bring them out into the light and give them fresh food and water. They begin to thrive immediately, even the weakest, one of the wild finches. I realize I now have an aviary and must care for them properly.

Birds are a symbol of soul or spirit. Wild birds, like the finches here, are symbols of a great creativity: untamed, part of nature. Two is the number of something new coming into consciousness. Here the wild spirit of creativity is captured and placed with a tamer version that has been contained. Both are rejected and left to die.

The creative spark is not extinguished easily, as the dreamer discovers when she goes to the closet and finds the birds still alive. She brings them out into the "light" of examination and gives them spiritual and emotional nourishment (food and water) so that they begin to thrive again.

The dreamer was a writer who did own two parakeets. Her issue was how she was defining herself as a writer. She was working as a freelancer, writing material for corporate clients. Though quite successful, she felt unfulfilled creatively. A deep part of her yearned to be a novelist. But fiction writing seemed very uncertain financially. Corporate freelancing paid well and was steady work.

In this dream, the dreamer saw that she was allowing a creative part of her to die in a dark closet, or unexpressed. She did not feel ready to give up the corporate writing, but instead made a commitment to devote a certain number of hours each week to fiction writing. In a year, she completed a short novel that was accepted for publication. The advance was not enough to enable her to quit corporate freelancing, but she felt very satisfied with her success. She started another novel. "Maybe at some point I can write only fiction, but at least I am now giving my creative voice a chance to speak," she said.

Part-Human Animals

Creatures that are part animal and part human also deserve our attention. Personification (as in putting human traits onto animals) is common in dreams, and is a potent way to put you in touch with the animal inside. Consider this part of a longer dream:

> . . . *There was a goat standing on two legs in the kitchen, cooking at the stove.*

Kitchens and food often pertain to spiritual transformation. This dream dealt with the dreamer's stubbornness concerning a relationship problem. The dreamer felt the dream was telling her she needed an awakening to see things in a different light. "I realized I was the goat," she said. "I was cooking up my own stew, or problems."

The next dream features a woman who is part snake and has the power of flight:

> *I was walking in a forest and I saw a snake woman. Not a goddess but a "normal" person who was "born this way." An incredibly thin woman (body like a snake, arms and legs like soft pencils) floating and undulating in the air like an eel in water. She had the face of a very beautiful East Indian woman. She crossed my way, not seeing me, and flew away.*

The snake woman has a sexual aspect (snake and eel). The dreamer was coming to terms with her sexuality and needed to feel it was "normal." She saw the snake woman as her normal sexuality. She comes into awareness of it (walking through the forest of the unconscious), sees that it is beautiful, but does not engage it.

Any dream animal can carry a message of spiritual import to the dreamer, but some animals have a greater association with the spiritual than others. For example, birds in general are symbols of the spirit. Certain birds, such as crows and ravens, which are very intelligent, are important messenger birds in mythology and folklore. Sea creatures—residents of the waters of emotion and the unconscious—also have strong spiritual associations. Dolphins and porpoises, masters of the sea of life, transport souls to the afterlife.

I dreamed I was on the edge of a cliff with my son (now thirteen but much younger in the dream) and was showing him the blue sea. Then we saw white things gliding close under the surface of the water: they were pelicans, lots of them, all swimming underwater to the left. Then one turquoise-colored sea-mammal rose out of the water like a dolphin, but I identified it as a big porpoise. We just sat there, admiring all those animals.

Pelicans are a symbol of Christ and the Christ spirit, for in order to feed their young, they sometimes prick their own breasts and use their own blood. Porpoises and dolphins also are Christ symbols. The turquoise color—a color of the gods—gives the dream a strong spiritual tone. The dreamer was at a time of spiritual transformation (the cliff overlooking the sea of life). This change had emotional associations with a change from earlier in life, represented by the age of the son in the dream. The animals symbolize spiritual enlightenment or support. They are just below the surface and breaking out to the surface, that is, coming into the dreamer's awareness of their presence.

Magical, Mythical and Supernatural Animals

Animals from the realms of myth, fairy tale and fantasy come into our dreamscape. They have unusual or magical abilities—such as the power of flight or the ability to talk. In the shamanic traditions, such animals are totems or power animals—real beings from the imaginal realm who come to aid us as helpers and teachers. As noted, dream animals in general are excellent message-bearers and teachers, but an added energy comes with the magical creatures. We may feel an expanded consciousness in their presence, or a spiritual nature to the dream.

I see a large white horse which may also be a unicorn, but I see no horn on it, just the knowledge that this is a horse of a divine nature. I hear that this horse has to be sacrificed by stretching a white string across his path while he's running so that he falls down. For a moment I become the white horse, running as fast as I can, and I see the white string stretching horizontally before me. I know what's going to happen but I feel absolutely no fear or pain about it. This has to be done, period. I black out for a moment, then I am myself again, standing by a table beside the severed and burnt head of the white horse. It is burnt and charred as if it had been in a strong fire. I lift it with both my hands, I shake it a bit and then I squeeze it as you'd squeeze a dried seed pod or an ear of wheat. It crumbles between my hand and a small quantity of wheat grains fall from it. I feel very satisfied and I say: "Fine; now all hungry people will have something to eat."

In mythology and folklore, the horse symbolizes mankind's base animal nature, instinct, nonhuman psyche and the unconscious. Thus, the horse symbolizes the instinctive, animal life within the body. Here the horse is spiritualized—it is white, of a divine nature, and possibly a unicorn. The unicorn is a symbol of spirit, and also female purity, chastity and virginity; moral values and strength; the Christ spirit; royal strength. In myth, the unicorn is softened by love in the lap of a virgin. It carries a healing stone beneath its horn.

This dream addresses sacrifice and change. From the sacrifice, something new springs forth. Wheat is a powerful symbol of rebirth and the power of the Mother Goddess to bring forth new life from death.

Horses also are symbols of the body and physical health. However, the dreamer felt that the white horse/unicorn's sacrifice represented a decision she had made about a relationship that would affect the course of her life. She was involved in a limbo relationship with a married man. He was not fully engaged emotionally with her, and was reluctant to make any changes in his life that would affect his availability. She did not want to end the relationship, even though at times she was emotionally distressed and physically depleted over it.

After much soul-searching, she decided to commit herself to this relationship, thus eliminating the potential for any other relationship to come into the picture. In a sense, this was a sacrifice of her female virtue and innocence. As the dream horse/unicorn, she runs willingly into the white string (thus crossing over an important line or barrier within her) to

make her sacrifice. She is following her heart, not her head,
which is severed, or cut off from further consideration.

The dream was full of healing energy to the dreamer. To her, the wheat symbolized the promise of something new and fruitful that would develop. The hungry people represented not only herself—at last she felt she would be nourished spiritually and emotionally—but also transcended to a larger perspective: "They clearly meant to me 'everybody in the world who's hungry and needs to be fed'—mankind in general," she said. It also pertained to her own need to be fed spiritually in the relationship. The dream renewed her optimism and hope.

The next dream features a luminescent blue phoenix, a mythical bird that rises from the ashes of its own destruction in fire, and thus represents rebirth and renewal:

I was walking outside my house in the evening, dusklike, just a faint hint of light outside, when the corner of my eye caught a glimpse of a low-flying bird, flying along the streambed. At first, I thought my eyes were playing tricks on me. The bird had a magical aura about him. It had sparkling light which emanated off his body as he flittered through the brush. The light was the first thing that caught my eye, but as I looked closer, I could see a beautiful turquoise glow within the light. I called to my husband, saying, "Oh, Tom, come quick and see . . . it's the Blue Phoenix!" He was busy working in a shed, and didn't come.

I watched the bird fly around. It landed in a few bushes, gradually making its way closer to me. With each landing, I could begin to see more definition in the bird's shape and size, and other colors were becoming clear. Then I yelled to Tom, "Oh, Tom, it's a macaw, or a parrot, must be somebody's pet who got lost."

Then the bird flew over to me and landed on my right shoulder.

I spoke in a parrotlike voice, saying, "Hello, how are you?" All the while, I was petrified, thinking this bird could claw or peck at me, and I would be defenseless against it, because it was enormous! It was bigger than any parrot or macaw I had ever seen.

I looked into the eyes of the bird, and I could tell it wasn't an ordinary house pet. I could see wisdom, longevity, and intelligence. I petted its breast of feathers in a loving way, once again saying more endearingly, "How are you?" and then the bird parroted me and said back (but not in my same voice), "How are you?" He then left my shoulder and flew over to where my husband, Tom, was. He entered the shed, and landed on Tom's shoulder. I got the feeling that the bird somehow knew that Tom was not going to stop what he was doing to come out and see him, so he decided to go into the shed, and make himself present before Tom. I once again used the words "Blue Phoenix" as I called out to Tom, letting him know the bird was on its way to the shed to see him.

When the bird was in flight, it was that illuminated turquoise. In fact, the color was so brilliant, I could not get back to sleep, because the color image was so intense in my memory after awakening. However, when the bird landed on my shoulder, I only remember seeing the colors red and yellow in its feathers. (When I awoke, I wondered if it had anything to do with the fact it landed on my right shoulder, the one which I am currently having an arthritic type pain in.) An old song was on my mind as I awoke. The title of the song is "Life Could Be a Dream, Sweetheart" and tells about going up to paradise.

The dream held a great deal of energy and power for the dreamer, who recorded it in her journal. Later she revisited the dream to look for new insights:

As I try to bring the presence of this incredible bird into my conscious awareness at this time, I can feel the emotion which I felt in my gut the first time he appeared. The first thought that came to me was my father, who passed away six years earlier. I tried to recall the voice of the parrot as he landed on my shoulder. I had spoken in a parrotlike voice, saying, "How are you?" The parrot had a vaguely familiar, kind voice with earnest desire to know how I was doing when he asked, "How are you?" with an emphasis on the word "you." I am now wondering, could this have been the spirit of my father? Only once did I dream about being with my dad since he died, and it was a very frightening dream, and I begged him never to scare me in that way ever again. I'm feeling a little chuckle well up inside of me as I write this because it would be like him to find another creative way to visit me and be close.

The color of turquoise was his favorite color, I believe, and he always wore "Aqua Velva" aftershave. The other thing which I felt was of interest was that the weight of the bird, and the prick of his claws on my shoulder, was somewhat uncomfortable. It is interesting to note it was the shoulder I was having pain in. This pain lasted for nearly nine months afterwards.

The other emotion that I recall is that I felt such awe. It was the same feeling as if I had witnessed a miracle, or the feeling one would have being visited by a great deity. It was a feeling of, "I am so grateful that I am being recognized by the almighty." It was very typical of me and my personality, for whenever I experience something that is a "sight to behold," I am never satisfied to just have this experience for myself, I always want to share it with a loved one, or friend. I seek out those experiences where others can be a simultaneous captive witness with me. I was feeling the disappointment that Tom was not sharing the same spiritual blessing with me, and that his interest was more in being a loner in the shed, doing his own thing, and not having interest in any of the beauty that was taking place outside his world.

As I examine the colors red and yellow, which were only seen in the bird while he was on my shoulder, I think of the fire element. Red I associate with blood, heat, passion, life itself, and yellow with the eternal yang energy which is projected by the sun. The world revolves around these two colors. The yellow, radiant heat from the sun is projected from the outside world, and the red is the radiant heat projected from the "inside" world. When we are red, flushed, and blood is coursing through our vessels enabling us to express (project and radiate outward), we are full of life. We are filled up, we can open our arms outward, stretch our heads upward toward the radiance of the yellow sun, and stand in awe of our existence. At that season, early spring, I was in grave need to have those elements brought to me, as I tend to lose a lot of my internal heat and passion over the long winter. Having just had the flu, and being stricken with deep coldness, I am able to see how I need to become a snowbird, and travel to the warm desert over the winter (or at least call upon the Blue Phoenix to visit me again every early spring to bring me his radiant heat!).

One final thought regarding the song "Life Could Be a Dream, Sweetheart," which I woke up singing. I examined the word "sweetheart," and wondered if there was anyone who ever called me by that endearing term. I realized that my dad was the only one who had ever called me sweetheart. Now I'm more convinced that he was the Blue Phoenix.

In dreamwork with animals, ask them what they have to say to you. Think of both their positive and negative associations. Your intuition will tell you which fit. Look up information on animals. An encyclopedia, for example, will tell you about their instinctual habits and behaviors. You may learn something new that sheds great light on your dream. Creatures who live in the depths of water or in the earth— such as snakes, lizards, fish, and rabbits—represent our unconscious or our inner underworld. Animals that live in two worlds—such as birds that swim on the water, like ducks and swans—mediate between the realms of the conscious and the unconscious.

Jung once observed that life is a continual adjustment between the conscious ego and the unconscious Self. Animals in dreams help us make those adjustments so that our true Self can emerge. The Self is the unifying principle within, the center that embraces both the conscious and unconscious. Animals are dream allies that can help us safely explore our inner depths and transcend to new heights of enlightenment.

ELEVEN

Insects

Most of our associations with insects are negative, for we have an ancient and collective revulsion and fear of them. Most people consider insects ugly, even evil-looking, and associate them with dirt, filth, abominations and demons. We call insects "pests." We have slang terms associating insects with undesirable things: we are "bugged" when we're annoyed and "buggy" when we're restless and irritable. If something or someone is "bugging" us, we are being pestered. "Bugged" also refers to surreptitious surveillance, an invasion of privacy.

In fact, invasion probably is the primary thing we dislike about insects. Singly or en masse, insects have the ability to invade our space and life and make things unpleasant for us. They bite, sting, chew and infest. Despite the advantage

of our size, we often feel at the mercy of these tiny creatures. They are masters of camouflage, they come out at
night when we are sleeping and off guard, they creep
through tiny openings, they crawl out from the dark under-
side of things, they attack us from the air. They have their
own agenda and intentions. We are not interested in understanding them or coexisting with them. Our immediate
response to them is a desire to eradicate them—wipe them
out of our way.

Despite our negative associations with insects, they frequently bear important and positive messages for us in
dreams. They definitely command our attention. They point
to things that are not good or right for us, and to things—
or even parts of ourselves—that are being neglected. Insects
literally represent what "bugs" us, and what we would like
to eliminate without having to think about it.

*There was something in the room I wanted very much but every
time I tried to enter I was stopped by a bug. It was* big*, sort of like
a locust, or a cicada, and was sitting on a small table. It would fly
at me, making lots of noise, giving off sparks, until I retreated. I was
terrified of it and gave up on whatever it was I wanted in the room.*[1]

The intention of the insect is to influence the dreamer
to give up whatever she wanted. It was on the table, perhaps
a matter or course of action still under negotiation with herself. The insect can be seen as cautioning her or warning
her away. Perhaps only something that scares and revolts
her—an insect—can sufficiently get her attention.

In dreams, insects often are associated with sexual matters. We may harbor unconscious fear and revulsion about

sex. In the following dream, a disintegrating marriage had led to a distaste for sex:

I am at a seaside resort alone. Everyone around me is having fun, and I drift about looking for something to do. There are people in boats who are cruising offshore reefs and islands; people at the beach and in the water; and people inside the resort hotel. I decide to put on a swimsuit and go to the beach. I get sidetracked at a shop selling beachwear and wonder if I should buy a little plastic necklace to go with the swimsuit. I am chagrined to have only a plain one-piece suit with me instead of a bikini that looks much better.

There is a scene in which I wade into the water, only to find eels swimming in it, and I get out quickly.

. . . There is another scene in which I am putting on black nylons, and find that dead flies are mashed into the legs of them and stick to me when I put the nylons on. I take them off and peel the flies off.

The dreamer was feeling increasingly alienated from her husband. The marriage had been deteriorating, and with it, sex. The lack of emotional intimacy made it more and more difficult for the wife to be open to the intimacy of sex. Yet she desired it at the same time. The seaside resort where everyone else is having fun represents the desire for intimacy and play. Everyone else is having fun but the dreamer, who is alone. Her feelings of sexual inadequacy are represented by the plain swimsuit. When she does enter the water, she is put off by the eels, symbols of the phallus and sexual contact. Black nylons suggest seductiveness and feminine sexuality, which is ruined by the dead flies. Flies are associated with aphrodisiacs ("Spanish fly") and the phallus,

which is hidden beneath a fly, or zipper. The sexual side of
the marriage had as much life and desirability for the
dreamer as the dead flies.

A dreamer who had conflicting feelings about sex had
the following dream:

*I am invited to a planning session by X. and Y. [business asso-
ciates]. I go to a small building that is a living quarters, like a dorm.
I am shocked to see that it is so squalid inside. There is water on
the floor, garbage everywhere, and it is so dilapidated and ram-
shackle that it is disgusting. I cannot believe that people (young
men, it seems) live there.*

*A young man appears in the doorway holding a cockroach the
size of a cat. In fact, it looks like a cat-rat: it is black with a cat's
ears, short fur and a rat's tail. With glee, he says he is going to set
this cockroach on me. He releases it and it comes after me. It seems
to be evil. I run, but it follows. There is snow on the ground—I seem
to be on a mountainside. I throw some snow on top of the creature,
covering it, and dash through the brush down the mountain. The
brush tears at me as I go.*

Due to childhood conditioning from her mother, the
dreamer had deep-seated beliefs that sex was "dirty" and
"not something that nice girls enjoyed." However, as she
gained independence and had her first sexual encounters,
she discovered that she really enjoyed sex. As a result, she
experienced an internal conflict over how she should regard
sex and how she should behave sexually. Her efforts to rationalize it are symbolized by the business planning meeting.
But the meeting is tainted by dirt. That the squalor belongs
to young men reinforces what the dreamer's mother told
her about "all a man ever wants."

The cockroach represents the dreamer's sexual fears and feelings. Its cat-like attributes symbolize feminine sexuality. The dreamer is pursued by her own sexuality seeking to be accepted, but which has been demonized as "evil." She tries to freeze it out with snow, a symbol of frozen emotions. If she does not allow herself to feel, perhaps it will go away. She is torn by this, however, represented by the brush tearing at her as she flees.

Another example of a cockroach representing sex is found in the next dream:

I have invited some people over to the house. It is the last minute and I have done no preparation for what I wanted to be an elegant affair. I set the table. There are two tables I can use. One is in the basement and a larger one is out on a deck. I seem to alternate back and forth.

A huge black cockroach crawls over the table. I am revolted and ask my husband to kill it, but he refuses to do so. He says it is his policy not to kill bugs. The cockroach jumps away like a cricket.

The guests are very late. I begin to think they won't come at all. I invited them for 9:30 and it is now 10:30. Suddenly they all come. They are impressed by the table setting. I ask if they would like Bloody Marys and they say yes. When I open the freezer to get the vodka, I see I have enough only for one or two drinks. The dream ends before they can discover the inadequate food I have prepared.

Food is a symbol of spiritual and emotional nourishment. The dreamer does not have enough to give out to others (the table on the deck) or even to herself (the table in the basement). The banquet is spoiled by the huge cockroach

that runs across the table, and which the dreamer's husband
refuses to dispatch.

The dreamer felt that this dream represented resent-
ments she harbored against her husband, which were affecting her sexual interest. She was attempting to suppress
her feelings by putting her attention into superficial enter-
tainments, which failed to truly nourish her (the impres-
sively set dinner party without enough food). The Bloody
Mary drinks symbolized her feelings that she was "bleeding"
emotionally.

Insects can be approached in dreamwork in the same
fashion as animals: look for your own resonances with qualities and characteristics associated with a particular insect.
For example, ants might symbolize industry, teamwork and
organization, or swarming (being overwhelmed). Bees likewise might symbolize industry and hard work ("busy as a
bee") or the ability to sting. A wasp might symbolize one's
own waspishness. Parasites can represent something that
is sucking away vitality or energy. Termites attack and de-
stroy from within a structure. Blood-sucking mosquitoes
sap vitality. Butterflies—one of the few insects we like—
can represent beauty and rebirth, especially from something
ugly or undesirable. The homely caterpillar spins a cocoon,
from which a beautiful butterfly emerges. Ladybugs, another of the few benign insects in collective opinion, represent luck.

Spiders are common in dreams. They can represent
craftiness and deceit, for spiders lay in wait for their prey.
In mythology, they are symbolic of time, for time is spun
like a web. In myth and fairy tale, spiders are associated

with witches and old, witchy women who possess a deep knowledge of nature. Jung associated spiders with a negative mother.

The following three dreams belong to a woman who has frequent unpleasant dreams involving spiders:

Dream 1:

I am in a house with a parlor like the one I have now. The ceiling is covered with cobwebs and cocoons of moths and pods of eggs of spiders. Some have already opened. There is a creaking sound as others open. I am aghast that I have allowed all this stuff to collect. I must get a vacuum cleaner and take everything off.

Dream 2:

A vivid dream. I am in a foreign place. I get dressed in my white linen shirt and tan chinos. I feel something under the shirt, like a big insect. I move around gently, so that I don't get stung or bitten, but it bites me anyway in the upper middle back. It then crawls out on my shoulder and I see that it is a black widow spider. I worry about the bite being fatal. I take off the shirt and turn and look at myself in a mirror. Drawn on my back, like with a black felt marker pen, is a spider web and a black widow off to the side of the web. In the center of the web, where I have been bitten, is a ring with coarse, long hair sprouting out of it. It is horse hair, like from a mane.

I look up black widow spiders in a reference book. The book, speaking in the first-person plural of "we," says that the only effect of the bite is terrible arthritis in old age. Fortunately, there is a new cane on the market to help with walking. So I won't die, but the effect of the bite is permanent, and I am doomed to old-age arthritis.

Dream 3:

I am at a hotel, where I have come for a meeting. My bed is a little cot that is pushed up against one wall. Above the bed is a shelf. The shelf is full of what appear to be clusters of ruby-colored crystals. Somehow I know that these crystals really are spiders, but I am not worried. I go to sleep. When I get up the next morning, I go to the closet to get my clothes, and discover that all of my clothes have been infested with little spiders, like eggs were laid and hatched out. Suddenly I realize that the ruby crystal spiders are not frozen, but very much alive, and I slept beneath them all night long! As soon as I realize this, I feel something crawling in my hair. I am infested with spiders. I am certain they will bite me. I wake up before they do.

The dreamer associated these dreams with her own negative mother, an issue she had been struggling with all of her life. Her mother was critical and always managed to see the negative side of any situation. Any good news or success experienced by the dreamer was immediately brought down. The mother constantly doubted the ability of the daughter to achieve much of anything. In her earlier years, the dreamer suffered from depression, lack of self-confidence and lack of self-esteem. She had a hard time finishing projects because her initial enthusiasm would be battered down with doubt and hopelessness.

In adulthood, the dreamer had invested a lot of time and energy dealing with this conditioning. The dreams reveal the extent of the "infestation." Spiders cover the ceiling of her house. A spider attacks her on the back (betrayal) and then lays in wait. Spiders masquerade as gems and then attack her during sleep. Spiders are in everything—clothing and hair. As in the second dream, she won't die from this negativity, but eventually it will paralyze her (the old-age arthritis). These and other spider dreams were of great help to the dreamer in therapy.

Sometimes working with plays on words around insects can reveal the meaning of a dream:

My inner arms are covered with hives. In the hives are small worms, squirming about. I pull the worms out, cast them off, brush them away, but there are so many and their number is increasing.[2]

The dream came at a time when the dreamer was experiencing a lot of difficulty with the man with whom she was living. The situation was on her mind a great deal and was, as she described it, "under my skin." The difficulty will not go away, but worms itself out into the open.

Being overwhelmed by a multitude of insects, especially poisonous or harmful ones, can symbolize having to deal with something very unpleasant, as in the next dream:

I am standing before an open cupboard, one my mother used to have. There is a small rectangular aquarium in it but it contains no water, and no fish. Instead, there is a jar, like a jam jar, filled with some translucent jelly, like rice pudding. I realize I forgot to seal the lid properly and now all sorts of larvae creep through this white stuff. I'm horrified and angry at myself for being so careless. I realize I have to get rid of the vermin, so I go and get a can of aerosol insect spray. I know this is strong medicine but I have to do it. So I spray just a little bit of chemical product into the aquarium, and I'm surprised to find out that only one light pressure has caused a tremendous result. For there are no longer larvae in the jar, there are big, jet-black insects, of several types. I see large cockroaches, centipedes, all deep black, and also a black scorpion. All those bugs twist their bodies in agony, they're mortally poisoned and are going to die—and they sure show it, they move in pain, expel some black matter like black smoke, and the white gel is starting to boil, bubble and smoke. I'm horrified and at the same time I feel comforted that I've managed to kill them and get rid of them forever. But I'm thinking: when they're dead, I'll have to lift the jar with my hands in order to throw the contents in the toilet. And that seems tricky. I'll cover my hands with cloth to protect them. Then I remember that in the jar there also are a couple of little fish, white dotted with black. I feel sorry for them because, with all that poisoned boiling and bubbling, they will be cooked. I promise myself to buy new ones.

This dream also contains the negative mother. Due to the dreamer's carelessness, the contained negativity escapes, but is never able to reach threatening proportions. Though the larvae quickly grow in size, the dreamer is able to eradicate them. The little white fish dotted with black seem tainted in this environment, but will be replaced with the new. For the dreamer, this dream, despite its ugly images, heralded a healing breakthrough for her, a release from emotional shackles of the past.

Dreams with insects often repulse us so much that we do not want to think about them or work with them. Yet, that is often why the insects are present: they have come into dreams to call our attention to something we'd rather not think about, rather not deal with. If the insects are attacking, stinging, biting or overwhelming in numbers, the message has more urgency.

It is helpful to place dream insects in perspective with their waking life counterparts: insects play an important role in maintaining the equilibrium of nature.

TWELVE

Food and Eating

Just as food nourishes the body, food in dreams nourishes
the soul. Eating in dreams often symbolizes the need for
emotional and spiritual nourishment and support, or the
receipt of them. If jobs and relationships are leaving you
unfulfilled, you may find yourself eating and eating in
dreams.

The recipient of the following dream had been involved
in a love affair with a married man for about two years. She
was often frustrated at the fact that the relationship did not
move forward, but remained the same. Her lover was emotionally and physically unavailable to her most of the time,
yet she was determined to stay in the relationship, confident
that she would win out in the end.

I am waiting for him in a small café where some unknown people are taking care of me, feeding me and being good to me in every way. I tell them that my lover will come and meet me soon. Then someone comes in, who looks like W., but it's only a ghost, a shadow. Not the real one. So I pay no attention to him and he disappears. Again, another ghost who looks like W. comes in. I pay no attention and the ghost disappears. Then, a third time, someone comes in, and that's really W. He's dressed all in black. He sits by my side and starts hugging me and kissing me very passionately, while I'm eating something. I think: "This is very nice, but I wish he'd let me finish what I'm eating first." Then I realize that we're overdressed, and we both take off our coats in order to be closer.

Her unavailable, uncommitted lover aptly appears twice as a ghost and finally "for real" but dressed in a somber black. As had been the case in the relationship, he wants passion when he is ready for it, regardless of what she is doing or what she wants. The dreamer is being nourished by outside sources. Her appreciation of that, and her focus on eating despite the amorous advances of her lover, reveals how hungry she is for genuine emotion.

The dreamer had another dream involving food. The setting of the dream is a luxury hotel:

There are some half-raw steak pieces scattered on the white-tile bathroom floor. I pick them up and throw them in the wastebasket but it's made of wire and the meat is dripping. I don't like that at all but I don't know what to do about it.

In this case, the dreamer made a health association with the half-raw dripping meat. The image had a primal, animalistic connotation. She was emotionally drained from the relationship and was beginning to feel physically drained as well. Tossing the meat in the wastebasket represented throwing away her vitality. She doesn't know what else to do but let it go. The steak, or what is "at stake," is scattered around the white bathroom. It stains the purity of the white. The bathroom represents a place of personal intimacy. She is only a piece of meat left over on the floor.

The next dream reflects another woman's unhappiness in her relationship:

I attend a conference. I walk through corridors filled with people dressed in costume, like they were going to a gala. There are food counters. I stop at one, with ice cream, and start gorging myself on vanilla ice cream with a hard chocolate shell. Then I step up on the counter and put my shoe in the ice cream. I keep eating the ice cream and chocolate.

Conferences symbolize education and learning; the dreamer needs to learn something about herself. Everyone is dressed up; that is, things are not what they seem—they are only a façade. The ice cream is an interesting symbol. It is soft and therefore feminine, yet it has a hard shell. It represents the emotional state of the dreamer, who has built a hard shell barrier around her, but remains soft on the inside. Many people find ice cream to be very satisfying emotionally, and the dreamer acknowledged that she sometimes ate big bowls of ice cream when she felt depressed. Stepping on the ice cream symbolizes her disdain for, and anger at, her depression and neediness—yet she keeps on eating. The need does not go away.

In the next dream, the dreamer is surrounded by food, but can't get what she wants:

I am at a banquet. There are long tables with all kinds of dishes of food. It is a buffet. The dishes are all side dishes—I have to place an order for main dishes. I order two main dishes, but through foul-ups they never arrive. Even though there is plenty to eat I am upset not to get the dishes I want.

The banquet symbolizes plenty and abundance. There is a great selection of food, that is, many choices. Furthermore, it is a buffet, which is serve-yourself and all-you-can-eat. Despite the abundance of food, none of the dishes are main courses. The food the dreamer really desires seems unobtainable.

For the dreamer, this dream represented her feelings of unfulfillment. She was in her thirties but hadn't found the right man. All of her relationships were just side dishes—she now wanted the main course of a permanent and committed relationship.

In the next dream, eating in fine restaurants is a symbol of success:

I am at a conference in Washington, D.C. I am trying to get myself known. I network the conference. There seems to be a lot of interest in eating out at fine restaurants. I know a few, but not the whole territory. I tell a paunchy man that Washington is much changed in restaurants. "A good meal used to be a steak and a baked potato, but things are a lot different now," I tell him. Somehow he is going to help me.

Suddenly I have an insight that I am going to "make it" in this town. I am going to be powerful. A celebrity. I know just what to do.

I go around to fancy restaurants and introduce myself to the maitre d's and give them my card. They will all know who I am when I walk in the door with others.

I awaken with the very strong feeling that I have made a turning point in consciousness. I am indeed going to make it big. I can do it. I will do it. It is possible. It is done.

The dreamer felt he was on the verge of a breakthrough in his career. He lived and worked in Washington, D.C., a town of networking, connections and business done in restaurants. Once again, a steak symbolizes what is "at stake," which is an upgrading of the dreamer's career and lifestyle.

The foods we eat in dreams also carry meaning. For example, eating fruits might mean something sweet, or bringing something to fruition. Meat can represent nourishment for energy. Eating fish can be seen as a way of connecting to one's inner core or intuition. Vegetables are basics, and often unexciting. In fact, we use vegetable terms to describe undesirable traits in people. Cabbage-heads are dull people, and couch potatoes are lazy and "vegetate." When someone has lost cognitive ability, we say they have become "a vegetable," implying that life has no meaning or value. On the other hand, however, a woman who is a "tomato" is sexually alluring.

But the lowly seeming vegetable can become powerful and magical in myth and fairy tale, such as the giant beanstalk that takes innocent Jack into another realm of consciousness.

In the next dream, dullness and boredom are symbolized by cabbages:

I am in prison, feeling hopeless. Long corridors stretch out like underground tunnels. Then it becomes a P.O.W. camp. The soldiers are listless and depressed. There are lots of browns, greens and grays, especially in their uniforms. I suddenly notice that their heads are all cabbages. It becomes a field of cabbages.[1]

This dream can be seen as pointing to boredom on the part of the dreamer, who feels hemmed in and limited. Everything in the dream, from the emotional state of the soldiers to the long tunnel-like corridors of the prison to the colors, are low in energy.

Although we associate vegetables with dullness and things we do not like, vegetables have deeper and more profound meanings as symbols. The root of the word "vegetable" means the very opposite of dullness and inactivity: to animate, invigorate, enliven, grow, refresh and vivify. The vegetable soul nourishes all living things in a cycle of birth, death and rebirth. Vegetation deities are associated with the mysteries of death and rebirth, and have certain totemic foods, such as corn, wheat, rice, yams, coconuts, breadfruit and taro root.

The vegetable soul grounds the rational soul and is the mediator between the conscious and the unconscious realm. It is dark and downward pulling, connecting us directly and intimately to our ancestral roots and to the roots of the earth and nature. In dreams, vegetables pull us down to our own roots. Jung observed that plants are nourished by the elements, and therefore the vegetable kingdom represents the very deepest level of the unconscious, where we encounter the roots of our real self, and where the fundamental life energy of all things originates.

In dreams, vegetables are seldom dramatic, but their ap-

pearance may have profound meaning. In the broadest
sense vegetables are a connection to one's family, community and ancestral roots. In the following dream, a man visits
his parents in their working-class neighborhood, after living
far away from them for many years:

> Some areas have been cleared and are like allotments. We own
> quite a few. They are roughly planted with vegetables. My parents
> are very proud of these plots. It's what they have acquired over the
> years, the family land, although I'm not sure it's officially theirs.
> Anyway, what a terrible place to have it—still the same old environ-
> ment and they aren't really growing anything. Same old pretentious
> but sad place.[2]

Despite the dreamer's disdain for his wounded family
roots, the family terrain has been changed with the addition
of vegetables—a slow but fundamental transformation that
in turn has changed his parents.

As seen in preceding dreams, eating vegetables signifies
the taking in of spiritual nourishment of the most fundamental kind; the subsequent process of digestion is the ab-
sorption and assimilation of this nourishment into the
psyche. Cooking vegetables is an alchemical process, an in-
dication of innerwork. Growing vegetables indicates fertility
and renewal. Rotting vegetables—a symbol of death—are a
precursor to renewal and growth. Seeing rows and rows of
neatly planted vegetables could mean immobility or fear of
immobility or a loss of will—or a sense of orderliness and
solid organization. Wild vegetables are disorganization,
chaos, things and relationships that are broken down. Frozen vegetables show a state of spiritual suspended anima-

tion. Processed vegetables have had some or all of their spiritual nutrients removed.

It is said that we are what we eat. In dreams, this is truth.

THIRTEEN

Houses, Buildings and Structures

Houses, buildings and other structures in dreams—such as towers and bridges—all bring information to a dream. Sometimes they are familiar to us—the house where we grew up, the place where we work—and sometimes they are foreign. They can represent parts of our lives, such as family relationships; work; emotional and mental states; states of consciousness; and sets of attitudes, which may either be holdovers from the past or active in the present. Women have more home dreams and family settings than do men, and also more indoor settings than men.

Houses, or homes, are personal: we live in them. They provide shelter, protection, comfort and status. Our most intimate needs and relationships take place in houses. We get conditioning, approval and disapproval at home. We dream about homes a lot.

Dreaming of being in the house where you grew up can relate to personal things from the past. Perhaps there are lingering relationship issues with family members, or old behavior patterns that need to be changed. The dream also may be evoking emotions from the past, perhaps a time when you were very happy or a time when you were very sad. These emotions might be present in your current life. How a home is furnished, and a home's overall condition, provide information. For example, a childhood home with a living room devoid of furniture might speak of emotional disengagement or disconnection. Wanting or looking for a new home can represent a desire for a change in relationships, or for a more comfortable emotional zone.

Every room in a house has its own significance, too. Bedrooms represent our most personal feelings and relationships. Bathrooms represent privacy. Kitchens, dining rooms and eating areas represent spiritual nourishment and spiritual change (cooking and ingesting). Living rooms and family rooms have connections to daily life and relationships, and family harmony. Basements often represent the subconscious, fears and anxieties, as in this dream about facing an uncomfortable situation:

I am put in a dark room as a test to face my fears of the dark. It is the basement. Those who are testing me will attempt to frighten me. Object: I must know what is fake and not be afraid. The test begins with obvious horror house–type gimmicks. Dream ends.

Attics can represent expansion of consciousness. Garages can be places where we keep practical things, or places where we store stuff we don't need but don't want to throw away. Looking through closets and drawers can represent rummaging through the past. Exploring new and unknown rooms symbolizes new awareness of self. Plumbing and leaking pipes and roofs can represent emotional issues.

The following are a selection of house and home dreams that illustrate many of these symbolic meanings.

NEW HOUSE

Sometimes we try to fix inner problems with an outer solution. For example, if we only had a new house, then everything wrong with the present life would be righted, as seen in this dream:

We find the perfect house at the perfect price. It is empty. Then we find a tape recording left behind by the owners admitting that the roof leaks in several places. The water isn't much—just a few ounces a year in drips. I am disappointed and no longer want the house. I do not want to try to fix the leaks, and even if the owners put on a new roof, I would worry about unseen water damage and rot to the wood within the frame.

When the meaning of this dream became apparent to the dreamer, it had a significant emotional impact. On the outside, her marriage looked perfect. She and her husband had glamorous jobs, nice children and an affluent lifestyle.

And, in fact, they were shopping to move up to a larger house. But inside, that is, on the emotional level, there was emptiness, created by a steady drip of deterioration of the marriage over time. The dreamer felt increasingly disconnected from her marriage, and filled her emotional emptiness with a busy schedule of outside activities. The leaks in the roof represented her weakening ability to hold back her true emotions. They were dripping in, not too noticeable, but nonetheless causing damage to the structure. The tape recording left by the previous owners seemed to indicate an unwillingness to be upfront about the problem—just like she ducked confronting her husband about her increasing unhappiness. The dream raised a question that she had to confront: did she want to stay in the marriage?

HOUSE IN DISREPAIR

A house in poor condition can point to problems in a dreamer's personal, or "home" life. The next dream was a repeating one for the dreamer, and had a nightmare quality:

The majority of my nightmares take place in this house. It is a mansion out in the country, very old Southern style. I have never seen this house, been to anything like this house, nor have I any relatives that lived in such a house (as far as I know; I have a large family). This is my nightmare house. Sometimes it is in its day, grand and beautiful, but the majority of the time it is almost demolished, overgrown with weeds, etc. It has a horseshoe driveway, there are more trees and such on the right side of it. It also has a big front yard. It is always haunted and only on a few occasions has someone

I've known lived in it. I am always trapped in it. Usually I am either trying to open or close a door, but some force won't let me. It's very cold and I usually get a strange smell. All kinds of different things occur in these dreams, but the house and its surroundings are basically the same. This house has been with me for as long as I can remember.

This nightmare house seemed to appear whenever something needed to be changed or resolved in the dreamer's life. Being trapped in the house represented her feeling stuck or unable to move forward—there was always "something" preventing her from doing so. The house appearing in grand condition represented the potential results of change. Weeds in the yard represented things that needed to be weeded out in her life. Sometimes the house represented old emotional issues that still "haunted" her. The nightmare house especially made appearances in her dreams when she realized she ought to let go of a long-term romantic relationship and make some career changes, but had taken no action on either matter.

In the next dream, a shabby house symbolizes lack and depression in the dreamer's life:

I am living in a house, not the one I currently know. It is sort of shabby and dingy—tired and outdated furniture and drab yellow-green curtains. I have invited some people over for brunch, but I don't have enough food.

The house had absolutely no appeal to the dreamer, and reflected her emotional state of being. She felt tired and leftover, like the outdated furniture. The yellow-green curtains seemed sickly. There was no spiritual nourishment (food) in the house. The dreamer acknowledged feeling severely depressed over the state of her life. She realized that things were not going to change by themselves; she would have to take action.

HOUSE ON FIRE

I dreamed that the house I live in was burning down. Flames were shooting out of all the windows. I was outside watching, along with a crowd of people. Nobody did anything to put the fire out.

The dreamer awoke with a curiously apathetic feeling about the burning down of her house. Fire is a symbol of purification; when a structure burns to the ground, the slate is wiped clean. For the dreamer, this symbolized her increasing apathy toward her marriage. However, she was reluctant to take action on her own to change her situation. Secretly, she had been wishing for some act of fate or God to come along and wipe her slate clean so that she could start over again.

OLD HOMES

Dreams of old homes, or dreams of homes involving people who are no longer a part of our life, can relate to the need to let go of the past or resolve something from the past in order to be able to move forward. Homes from certain time periods may represent attitudes in the dreamer. For example, a Victorian home may represent conservative values, formal or stiff manners, or repressed sexuality. It

could also represent a desired state of being, such as ele-
gance.

The next dream features a large and impersonal house, not one known to the dreamer. Rather, it seems to be a gathering place for learning.

I am somewhere in a big house with many people, and I feel I am there only for a short time, like for a gathering or a course or something. M. [ex-husband] is there and I am hoping to get back together with him. He is happy but oblivious to my intentions. Things happen so that I never have a chance to talk to him about it, and suddenly I realize that it is never going to happen. I know I will love him forever but going back is not possible.

Then I see a door. It is purple, a dark purple, with a shining gold knob. As I look at it the door recedes away from me into the blackness of space, until the gold knob becomes a dot and then is lost in infinity.

Though the dream house was not identifiable to the dreamer, it did remind her of a place where she had once attended a summer learning institute. She took the setting in the dream to mean that she needed to learn something. She had indeed been regretting her divorce and fantasizing about getting back together with her ex-husband. It wasn't feasible, and the divorce had been the right decision. But her life felt stagnant and empty. Meanwhile, her ex-husband moved on with his life.

In the dream she never has a chance to act on her longing, and she does realize that though she will always have a love for him, going back is not the answer. The past is past.

A symbol of hope, change and new beginning then appears in the dream as the purple door with a shining gold knob. Doorways are symbols of change. Purple is often associated with the spiritual and intuition, and gold represents enlightenment and spiritual treasure. The door recedes into space. The dreamer felt that it represented the future, and the meaning of it receding was that she needed to do much work on herself before she was ready to go to the door. It had a powerful effect on her, filling her with positive thoughts and energy about all the possibilities that lay before her. She needed to look forward, not back.

In the next dream, a childhood home is the setting for a dream about letting go of the past:

I am living in the house of my childhood. My husband is there. Mom is not. The house is filled with people from my near and far past, who are visiting and staying over. I am happy. As I hang my clothes in my old closet, I think, "I think I'll just stay here." I gather it was supposed to be temporary, but I decide to remain permanently.

A Voice says to me, "You can't."

I ask why not. The Voice says it is not an appropriate house for the things I have to do, the people who must come to see me. I answer that I'm going to stay anyway.

The dreamer was a young woman who had recently made a long-distance move required by her husband's change in jobs. She had never before lived far away from her hometown, and she felt homesick. She was especially attached to the house of her childhood. After her father died, she had spoken to her mother about buying the house from her, so that she herself would have it to return to someday.

The dream reflects these longings. Then her Higher Self

comes in as the "Voice" and tells her this regression is neither appropriate nor possible. She has other things to do in life. In the dream, she remains determined to go back. However, in her dreamwork she realized that what the dream was telling her was true: she could not go back to a life that was over.

HOUSES THAT REPRESENT CHANGE

A common dream is to be in your house and discover that it is under renovation or has new and unknown rooms. Such dreams can occur when personal life changes are underway, or seeking to begin. The rooms that are changing can provide valuable insight into the areas of life that need attention.

A divorced woman who had recently remarried had this dream:

I live in a large mansion made of stone. A woman comes to stay with me. She is older, small and dark-haired—not someone I know in waking life. Instead of giving her a guest room, I decide to offer her my own room. I offer to show her around the house. Every time I describe it verbally, it acquires more rooms, especially bedrooms. I tell her there are four bedrooms in one place, and when we get there, we find five. It is as though I don't even know my own house. As I take her around, the house becomes cavernous, like an airplane hangar or one of those warehouse stores. Much of it is empty. There is a lot of remodeling work going on—walls being put up to create rooms out of the cavernous space. I tell her a man has purchased the house and is remodeling it.

The dreamer recorded the following notes in her dream journal about what the dream meant to her:

I am made of stone, which has a feeling of coldness, hardness, fixedness. It is strong but cold. There are huge empty spaces inside me—and spaces I didn't even know about. I don't even know my own inner self. The man must be J. [new husband], though he is offstage. In our marriage he has "purchased" my personal life, and our relationship is literally remodeling my inner space. The creation of rooms from empty space brings definition, warmth, activity. The woman who comes to stay might represent an integration with, or welcoming of, a new feminine energy. Number of bedrooms: from four (foundation, fixedness, the known old self) to five (the number of change). Bedrooms represent personal intimacy.

In her previous marriage, the dreamer had felt emotionally dead and disconnected from her femaleness. There was an emotional vacuum within. She was not "at home" in her marriage. She felt completely the opposite in her new marriage. She felt the dream was a positive sign of inner healing.

In the next dream, the foundation of the house symbolizes the foundation of a marriage:

R. and I have our house moved off its foundation to make repairs in the foundation. I'm concerned that the contents of the house will be stolen, even though the house is under guard.

I am astonished by the foundation. It isn't what I expected at all. It consists of piles of giant pillows (covered with black-and-white-striped ticking) covered by a thin layer of concrete. The foundation is incomplete in one spot where a porch was enclosed. There is nothing but a hole there.

I'm afraid that the foundation will not be put back together correctly, but the young man doing the repairs (a neighbor in real life) doesn't seem concerned.

This dream occurred after the dreamer and her husband decided to seek counseling together to repair a rift in their marriage. The counseling was requiring them to examine the foundation of their relationship. The wife was unsettled by what she thought was revealed in the process (it wasn't as solid as she thought) and worried that the relationship would not be put together right as a result of the counseling. She associated the real-life neighbor with skill and competence. He was, in fact, a carpenter who worked on houses. She read the dream message as reassurance that the skill and competence of their counselor would help them make the necessary repairs.

Dramatic personal growth can be symbolized by spiritual symbols in a house or living quarters, as in this dream:

I find myself showing some extensions of my apartment to the lady who lives next door to me. Some extensions are long, and there is a huge, beautiful, high stone chapel, baroque style, built in delicately sculpted naked gray stone but without any other ornaments. The vault is very high and lit with very bright oval windows. I'm a bit embarrassed to let this lady know that my lodgings have this luxurious, divine extension. We enter through one end of the chapel and there's another exit at the other end, on the west side, but it's closed with huge green gates. In the southwest corner, near the large gates, I find a smaller, open gate leading into a very orderly, old-fashioned garden that looks like a small urban park. It has some old, dark-foliaged trees—horse-chestnut trees, cedars, pines and yews. One end of the garden is separated from a graceful urban landscape (the Place de la Concorde in Paris) by large glass panels and other trees. There is a wide flat marble bench that can be used to look at the city.

As I get out of the garden, I see a bush of bright red flowers—

peonies in my dream but they rather look like hibiscus. The flowers are ready to bloom out, but they look kind of dried up and burnt on the outside. And I wonder if they'll be able to open up. . . . Suddenly I am holding in my hand the bottom part of a broken plastic bottle filled with a small quantity of water. Some voice tells me that this is divinely pure water, with strong magical properties, and that it can revive and regenerate anything.

So I decide to water my peony bush with this. As I start pouring it onto the roots, I realize that there is actually so much water (it flows abundantly, like a spring) that I can smother the plant in it. This will certainly save it and cure the flowers. There's even some water left for me: I drink some and wash my face with it. It is delicious and fresh, wonderfully clear, and I feel very lucky.

The dreamer had had some transforming experiences of a spiritual nature, and was pursuing spiritual study. This greatly expanded her inner house, represented by the grand chapel with its vaulted ceiling (a symbol of spiritual thoughts and consciousness). The neighbor woman represented a part of her that was still uncertain about her inner changes, and hence a source of some embarrassment to the dreamer. She still had to wonder that such grand experiences could happen to her.

Like doors, gates are thresholds to change, especially when gates open to beautiful gardens, also symbols of spiritual consciousness. The peony/hibiscus flowers symbolized the divine feminine, a nurturing quality that still needed to be awakened in the dreamer (the flowers were unopened and somewhat dried up). The nourishment came from special, divine water, a symbol of spiritual inspiration and nourishment, and the dreamer's own emotions. Her spiritual study had opened her up emotionally, and she was often

flooded with feelings of joy and love, and wanting to give
to others. The source of her spiritual nourishment was unlimited. Drinking it symbolized taking the nourishment into
her being at a very deep level; washing in it symbolized
purification. The happiness felt in the dreamer mirrored the
dreamer's emotional state in waking life: joy and optimism,
and feeling blessed.

In the next dream, the house undergoes changes by the
dreamer's own decorating:

*I am decorating a large house. I don't know if it is mine or some-
one else's. An older man is in charge—I must have his approval of
what I do. It is a handsome house with many rooms . . . very big . . .
and has high ceilings. It seems to go on and on. There is a question
as to what rooms will serve what purpose. I am to decide.*

*I set to work. I choose the colors. The decorating is not so much
drapes, etc., but more like an exhibit of mounted photos and art and
blocks of text. I consult the man along the way. Basically, he ap-
proves.*

In her dream journal, the dreamer recorded these observations:

*The big house represents my new life that is stemming from my
career change. It is beautiful in and of itself and has limitless potential for added beauty, depending on what is put into the rooms. The
choices are all mine. The end product is review, but not for success
versus failure.*

The dreamer was taking charge of her life by making an
important career change, to become self-employed as a consultant. She hadn't yet fully "owned" the new symbolic

house. But with its high ceilings, big rooms, many rooms and rooms of uncertain purpose, it showed that there was much potential ahead for expansion and growth. All the decisions were hers about what the house would look like. The photos and blocks of text were reminiscent of museum displays or exhibitions, which the dreamer associated with accomplishment, especially for others to see. The older man who had the final approval represented her inner masculine authority—the rational, logical side that keeps things on track and in focus. The dream was telling her that she could keep the creative and rational needs of her new career in balance.

HOTELS

Hotels are a temporary and impersonal substitute for homes. They serve people in transit. Hotel dreams may indicate we don't wish to stay in a place or relationship; perhaps we are not committed, or fear others are not committed.

This dream came to a woman who had been involved in a relationship for several years. She was committed to it, but her partner had never expressed a definite and permanent commitment to her.

I dreamed I was staying at a luxury hotel, in a large, ornate room. Half asleep in bed, I was thinking of the moment when I'd have to pay the bill, which would certainly be very expensive. I thought I could afford it, though.

I also sleep outside of my room, in a small orange bed placed in a corridor where everybody, clients and staff, keeps coming and going. A young woman in a tulip-shaped orange coat is anxiously asking for room service to iron her coat.

Then a Native American man passes by me and we look at each other while I am in bed. I lean on my elbows and he turns around and we start to talk. He's middle-aged, handsome and friendly, he wears a pair of brown jeans, a dark blue shirt, and a leather hat. He's carrying a branch of hazelnut buds in his left hand. He looks at me and says: "You're a very loving person. You were born to love."

"How can you see that?" I say.

"Your eyes, lady, I see it in your eyes."

And then he adds: "You have been exploited by many men who haven't given you much in exchange. However, the man you love now will." He went on to tell me a lot of detail about P., but I forgot the details when I awoke.

The luxury hotel symbolizes something with a high price: a relationship that may not end in commitment. This price worries the dreamer, but she feels she can deal with it when time comes for the account, or relationship, to be settled.

The impermanence of her situation is further emphasized by the fact that she does not even sleep in the room, but in a corridor outside the room, where she is potentially in the way of others.

The uncertainty of commitment wastes both the dreamer's passion and health. Fatigue is reinforced by the orange bed and the woman who wants her orange, tulip-shaped ("two lips") coat ironed. Orange is a color associated with sexual and personal power. Meat is full of iron. The dream came at a time when the dreamer felt both physically and emotionally depleted. Her partner has all the power in the relationship.

The Native American wise-man figure represented spiritual wisdom for the dreamer, giving her a message from her Higher Self. Her eyes, the "windows to the soul," speak of her intense desire to be loved, yet she has had unsuccessful relationships. The dream reassures her that her current lover does love her. Her faith in the relationship was renewed.

Buildings and Other Structures

Buildings are more impersonal than homes and often relate to work, or even to things we need to "build" in life. They can represent the personal and home life, but may indicate a detachment. Like houses and homes, they can represent sets of attitudes. Some have obvious symbolic meaning. Prisons and jails, for example, symbolize whatever is making us feel confined, stuck, trapped or imprisoned. Hospitals represent the need for healing, or a healing process that is underway, especially if one goes to a hospital and is treated.

In the following dream, the dreamer associated a commercial building both with her inner self and with her professional life:

A building located at the center of my hometown is rotated and totally gutted down to the bare beams/basic structure. It sits in this empty condition for a time, then plans are drawn for a major renovation and the building is totally remodeled and much improved by doing so.

The dreamer, knowledgeable about astrology, made these associations:

I associate that building, which is in my hometown, as being the center of town both literally and figuratively. It is located right at the intersection of the two main streets, which is considered the town's center point, and has also served over the years as a place of central activity for the town. I immediately associated it, upon waking from the dream, as representing the deep, core center of my being—the Self in Jungian terminology. For the past eighteen months I have experienced a Pluto transit to my sun. The sun represents the core essence of our being (our center) and Pluto, among other things, relates to getting to the deepest levels of clearing/death and rebirth.

This dream came midway through the transit's influence and clearly explained what I was experiencing . . . and helped me surrender to the process! And believe me, I do feel like I was gutted and renovated. Time now for the building to be "open for business," or in other words, my energy now seems more free to go outward into the world after being so pulled into the deep interior for restructuring!

As I write this I just got another insight of the significance of it being a commercial building, rather than a home. Now in hindsight of the past eighteen-month process, the deep Plutonian core shifts seem to be related to my professional life/identity (a commercial building) rather than my personal life, which would be more likely to be represented by a home.

TALL BUILDINGS AND TOWERS

Tall buildings and towers can represent changes in consciousness. Going up a tall building can symbolize spending a lot of time in mental activity—we're literally up in the tower of our head. What goes up must come down eventually, and descending from the heights represents a return to earth, to a reconnection with emotions, or to relating to the outside world in a more tangible, and less abstract, way. Life is a continual shifting of emphasis from one mode to the other. Sometimes towers in dreams represent withdrawal and isolation. We might seek out a tower to withdraw from the world, or because we think we are "higher" than everyone else.

After a long and intense period of research for a book, which involved a lot of mental activity and left-brain thinking for organization, presentation and so on, I had this dream:

I am in a building at least 300 floors high. I ride the elevator down from the 300th floor with a man. I remark that I have never done something like that before, ride down 300 floors. The elevator goes very fast, then slows for a while, and then picks up a little more speed before coming to rest on the ground floor. It seems maybe other people get on somewhere in the lower floors.

The dream seemed to address my shift in orientation. I related the building to my professional activities. I had spent a prolonged period up in the intellectual tower (symbolized by the 300 floors) and was in the process of coming back to earth, symbolized by the elevator ride. The man riding with me is my own animus, the logical, left-brain thinking we associate with the masculine. It was a good thing I was not leaving him behind, as one needs both animus and anima to function well in the world. The entry of other people into the elevator car symbolized a reconnection to people. When I am deep into a book I can be very isolated from others. The elevator coming to rest on the ground floor said to me that I was "grounded" again.

If the elevator had become stuck or had traveled very

slowly, I probably would have interpreted that as a sign that I needed to take action to help the process. Or, I might have asked myself if I was reluctant to leave the mental tower.

Here is another tower dream:

I was on the roof of a high observation tower to see the view. There were others with me and we were going to stand outside by resting our feet on the gutter and leaning back against the roof. Someone apparently brought up the question of whether the gutter was sound enough to hold us. I seemed to escape from this whole situation by going up into another higher observation tower to show the way to many people.[1]

The dreamer was a talented man who considered himself to be "above" the average person. He had recurring dreams of being high up, looking down on the view. The dream reinforced his feeling that it was his job to show others the way.

PUBLIC BUILDINGS

Structures that are open to the public may have an impersonal meaning to the dreamer, or indicate a need for privacy or the setting of personal boundaries. A common dream theme is to be living out your private life on display in a department store. People bustle around you but don't pay any attention to what you're doing.

My living quarters are contained within a department store, on the ground floor. I sleep on a hide-a-bed near the cosmetics and

*jewelry sections. If I'm asleep when the store opens, people walk
around me as if I'm not there. Nobody pays me any mind.*

For the dreamer, this dream spoke to her low self-esteem: she has no particular value to the store or the people in it. The phrase "as if I'm not there" was particularly meaningful, for she often felt that nobody would miss her if she were to suddenly disappear. The hide-a-bed also represents her low self-esteem—but the cosmetics and jewelry symbolize a desire to dress up her life, at least superficially. The dream was an eye-opener, and paved the way for some healing therapeutical work.

Department stores and shopping malls also represent choices. A dream set in a mall might be pointing out to the dreamer who sees one or few options that many choices exist.

In the next dream, a fancy store turns into a labyrinth, taking on a deeper spiritual meaning for the dreamer:

*There was a fine store. I wanted to get in and buy something, I
don't know what, but could only walk around on the outside because
the store seemed to be in a sort of shell. I wanted to get something.
I thought I wanted handkerchiefs. Then I thought I simply wanted to
get to the center of the store, which was a sort of labyrinth, but I
kept going around the edge. Then I came to a place where there
were various things, but it was time to go. I got onto a bus, but
instead of it going where I hoped, it turned into a side street and I
was vainly trying to stop it when I woke up.²*

The dreamer saw the fine store as a symbol for herself. There was something she wanted to reach or discover within her depths at her very center, but an outside shell prevented her from entering. Rather than persevere, she opts for a preprogrammed route (the bus) which doesn't take her where she wants to go. The dreamer also noticed that she used the word "wanted" four times. She did free association and came up with this sequence: "want to—want a—wanna—Wannamaker—want to make a—a creator—a maker—one who builds or makes something worthwhile—a wish to be a maker." The dream was pointing her to the creativity within her own depths. "I have a feeling that that is the inner me," she said.

FOURTEEN

Transportation and Traffic

Traveling in dreams tells us a great deal about how we are traveling through life: our direction and purpose; our speed; our ease or difficulty of making the trip; our comfort; obstacles and so on.

Automobiles, Difficult Roads and Getting Lost

Cars dominate the Western dream landscape. It's not surprising. We in the Western world spend a lot of time in our cars. We make statements with our cars about ourselves and our stations in life. The automobile has acquired an archetypal presence as a symbol for the ego self, which is the vehicle in which we drive around life. Jung observed that

automobiles represent how we move forward in time and
live our psychological life.

Common themes involving cars are driving out of control, getting lost, forgetting where you parked, letting someone else drive, and having your car break down. All of these are apt metaphors for how we drive through life. We aren't always managing the direction of life as we should; we get distracted and lose interest in things; we sometimes suddenly realize we don't really want what we thought we did; we let others make decisions for us, and we don't take care of ourselves or think well of ourselves.

A husband and wife shared this exact same dream about their car going out of control one night. It is recounted by the wife:

My husband and I were in a car, a little blue car that sort of resembled a bug, the old style, but not quite a bug. There were others in the car but they weren't really there, just a presence of others, you know, a feeling, like they were just along for the ride kind of thing.

We start out and we are in an area that is populated but not heavily and we are going up and down this hilly road and it has a few gentle turns. We are going along, we seem to be happy just going along, and then all of a sudden we don't have any brakes, the car doesn't run away or anything, we just keep going and going and we aren't really scared, but we realize we need to stop the car and we do at the bottom of the next hill. We just sort of turn the car into a slope or mound of loose dirt and it comes to a stop. Nobody is hurt or anything and that is how it ended for both of us. We had this dream the same night and for days it stayed with me. I think the fact that we had the same dream was more impressing than the dream.

As discussed in Quick FAQs About Dreams in chapter 1, people do "mutual dream," that is, have the same or similar dream on the same nights. This especially occurs among people who have an emotional rapport or bond with one another. The husband and wife were deep into a spiritual discipline that was having a profound effect on their lives. They were just enjoying the ride without paying much attention to where they were going. The car plowing into loose dirt is a symbol for getting grounded. The message they saw in this dream was to get in gear and pay more attention to what they were doing and where they were going in their new direction.

"In the last few years we have gone through massive reconstruction," said the wife. "It has been fun but sometimes it turns our world topsy-turvy, and we are always looking for ways to get through it just a little easier. We are constantly struggling to stay grounded and connected."

The auto in the next dream won't perform according to expectations, and then goes out of control:

I'm in a barren, desert-like place with hills and valleys. There are ancient ruins around me. I'm driving a car that doesn't seem to have much power. It won't climb the hills. I get near the top and then roll backwards. The scene changes and I'm driving at enormous speed along a precipitous drop. People I pass shout warnings at me to slow down, but I can't. I'm afraid I'm going to go over the cliff.

The dreamer felt besieged by conflict and stress, represented by the barren desert and ruins. He just wanted to get clear but was not able to, as symbolized by the low-powered car. Every time he felt he was making headway, he suffered a setback. The stress of this sometimes made

him feel that he was "just going to go over the edge" if
something didn't change drastically. The dream represented
how he felt emotionally—out of control and powerless to
change his situation.

The next dream also deals with navigating hills. Driving
up and down hills in dreams is a common dream drama.
Hills represent challenges, difficulties and obstacles—and
also changes in consciousness.

*I was driving in an automobile down a steep hill and had to pass
another car which was on my right, with a steep precipice on my
left. I just managed to get by. Then I had to go down to a bridge
with a sharp right turn beyond it and had a great fear of meeting
another car.[1]*

The key phrase for the dreamer in this dream was "I just
managed to get by." He often found himself in a "tight
place" where options seemed extreme (squeezing by or falling off a precipice). A bright and capable man, he had scattered his interests across many fields, and often thought he
would do better in life if he limited his focus. He was
strongly motivated to succeed in whatever he undertook.
The descent from the mountain (a lofty perspective) can be
seen as a change in consciousness, a return to more mun-
dane concerns.

A man in one of my workshops had repeating dreams
involving cars with two main themes. In one, he always
found himself riding in the backseat. His parents were in
the front seat and his father was always driving the car. In
the other, he would be leaving work and walking through the
parking lot, and suddenly forget where he parked his car.
Both of these repeating dreams concerned the way he was

living his life. He had entered a profession in order to please his parents, especially his father, and undertook many tasks and activities with parental approval in mind. He really wasn't interested in his work, which was represented by his forgetting where he parked his car. His true interests were elsewhere.

Cars replaced the horse. Like the horse in dreams, cars sometimes represent the physical body and our health. A broken-down car can point to a health problem, which might be physical or emotional.

> *I'm driving by myself on a long trip and my car keeps breaking down. I get out and find something, like a bumper, has fallen off. I get out a hammer and nail it back on. This happens several times.*

The dreamer was emotionally exhausted but refused to acknowledge to anyone that she could use some help and support. She felt that she was breaking down, but tried valiantly to keep up appearances that everything was fine. She wasn't doing the right thing, however—you can't fix a car with hammer and nails. It will keep falling apart.

Automobiles that have recognizable features that date them to a time period can relate to the past, as in the next dream:

> *I wake up hearing a noise outside our house, like someone pounding on metal. I look out the bedroom window and see a pack of young men with clubs bashing our prize car, a Cadillac from the 1960s. I am sickened to see them destroying our car, but I am afraid to do anything. If they see me watching, they might come into the house and attack us.*

The dreamer and her husband did own a vintage Cadillac from the 1960s and took good care of it. The dream did not reflect any fears of damage happening to it. Rather, it evoked emotions of helplessness and vulnerability on the part of the dreamer due to circumstances in family relationships. The vandals in the dream represent anger: angry behavior of others toward her, and repressed anger within her at them and at herself for putting up with their behavior. She had experienced the same feelings years before, during the time period of the car, in a similar situation. The dream helped her to examine her responses to the stress, and to avoid mistakes she had made in the past: being afraid to take action to stop abusive behavior.

Damaged cars can also represent damaged relationships:

My husband and I are on a trip and the car breaks down. I get angry, telling him that if he had taken care of the car in the first place, this wouldn't be happening. He ignores me.

The dreamer described her relationship as being like the car: broken down and unable to go the distance. She blamed her husband for the breakdown of the marriage, and felt that he ignored her concerns. In her dreamwork, she conducted a dialogue with her husband and with the car. It provided an opening for her to initiate honest communication with her husband about what they should do to rebuild their relationship.

Airplanes

Dreams in which we are flying planes are similar to automobile dreams. A common theme is to find yourself in the cockpit at the controls of a plane, when suddenly something goes wrong, fails or falls off, and the plane begins to go down. Such dreams can relate to us "flying high" and not paying attention to details; or needing to come back to earth; or expending too much energy so that we are in danger of crashing.

I'm flying a plane that's going to Chicago. Everything is fine, and then the plane suddenly starts shaking and a red warning light comes on. The nose tilts down. I try to regain control, but I realize we are going to crash. The dream ends before we do.

The dreamer was not a pilot. In the dream, it felt perfectly natural for him to be flying the plane. In waking life, he had been offered a job in Chicago. It was a tempting offer from a high-flying start-up company in high technology. He had reservations, but set them aside. The dream, with its warning light and imminent crash, caused him to reexamine his true feelings about the offer. He realized he would be happier in a job with less risk and more security.

Boats and Ships

Ships are ancient symbols of the journey through life and beyond life. They ply the waters of the unconscious and of emotion. They are not a personality symbol as much as automobiles, but they do tell us how we are faring on our trip through life.

I have repeating dreams about us being in a ferry boat and floating around, but we always wound up back at the terminal. It was a

Floating around means going nowhere. The dreamer and her husband always wind up at their starting point, which is a parking facility. The dream showed a lack of focus and direction. Ferries are piloted by someone else to get people from point A to point B. The couple wasn't certain of their goals, and so they "went nowhere" and "parked."

Ships and boats often represent major events or issues in life. Consider how we use ship imagery to describe important things. We say someone's ship sank or went down when a person suffers a disaster or tragedy. Our plans get "torpedoed," or destroyed by events or the actions of others. If we "miss the boat," we misjudge and miscalculate in a major way to lose out on an opportunity. All of these metaphors appear in dreams.

Sometimes our "boat" is nothing more than a raft or a piece of driftwood. Both of these evoke images of clinging to something for survival. Perhaps they represent all that's left of the wreckage of something in life.

Trains, Buses and Mass Transport

Trains, buses, subways, trams and other forms of mass transportation often represent following a track or predetermined path. We are part of the masses, not making our own trail. We are dependent on time schedules and routes set by others. These symbols can relate to self-expression and conformity. Missing a train or bus (or airplane) is similar to missing a boat—you're not on board when the action gets going. A question to ask in dreamwork is, "What am I doing in waking life that distracts or prevents me from moving forward?"

Theater critic and playwright William Archer recorded this dream:

A very frequent type of dream. I was at a place I conceived to be Watford Junction and wanted to get to London. I saw a train about to start, which seemed to consist entirely of one very splendid car de luxe. I made up my mind that, cost what it might, I would go by it, and produced a "wad" of American money wherewith to take my ticket. But just as I got to the ticket office a queue of other people suddenly appeared at it. I thought of pushing in ahead of them, but dismissed the idea, and fell into my proper place, with the result that the train started without me. Then another more ordinary train came in, and I asked an old man who seemed to be a servant of the company whether it was bound for London. He said "I don't know—that's what comes of democracy—no one knows anything." And I gathered that the company, or at any rate the station, was run on some collectivist (perhaps Soviet) system which resulted in complete disorganization. Then I made a rush over the metals to get into this train and succeeded in doing so, only to find that it started in the wrong direction. I remember no more.[2]

As Archer mentioned at the start, he had this dream frequently, with some variations. It contains day residues from the news and politics of his time. He interpreted the dream as symbolizing mental and physical obstacles in his life. He wanted things to be first-class and "de luxe," but had difficulty bringing that goal into being. In the dream, other people (obstacles) mysteriously get ahead of him in line. There is disorganization at the station. He gets on another, lesser train (makes a choice) only to find it will take him in the opposite direction of where he wants to go. Sometimes we make decisions—usually impulsive ones—that not only work to our disadvantage, but, like Archer's train, take us in the opposite direction.

The next dream involves a bus:

The location of this dream seems to be the waiting station of a bus line or street car line. I was waiting for a bus but somebody told me they wouldn't stop there and let me get on. There were some other men waiting. I thought the matter over and then walked down the line some distance so as to jump on before the bus got to the station. I did that and found a seat. Then as we passed the station the other men jumped on, but had to stand up.[3]

The dreamer was a man who did not consider himself to be competitive, nor had he been competitive in school and work. The dream, however, was urging him to do otherwise. He observed, "It looks to me as if my brain had figured out something while I was asleep. The secret of success in modern life is to be ahead of the other fellow and do it first!"

Streets and Traffic

Navigating busy streets, either on foot or in a vehicle, can represent hazards and obstacles, especially unexpected ones. In the next dream, a man on foot crosses a busy intersection:

I crossed diagonally in the midst of heavy traffic, where two streets intersected, but made my way through rapidly and easily. As

I got up on the sidewalk I had a feeling of pride for a moment, then realized that it wasn't a very important matter except that it illustrated a principle. I said to myself: "It all depends upon how you value the direction in which the road leads."[4]

The dreamer was a concert violinist. "In my early concert career I often had a feeling of incompleteness, of never quite putting over what was inside of me," he said. The dream addressed the many and often confusing roads to a goal. "The emphasis of the whole dream seems on the importance of knowing one's own mind," he said.

There is a reassuring element in the dream, too. The dreamer easily navigates the obstacles to reach the sidewalk.

FIFTEEN

Landscapes and the Elements

The four elements of nature—water, earth, fire and air—have their own symbolic meanings and give added dimension to dreams. Since ancient times, the elements have been ascribed masculine and feminine attributes and other qualities. For example, the feminine elements are earth, which is cold and dry, and water, which is cold and moist. The masculine elements are air, which is hot and moist, and fire, which is hot and dry. In dream language, these characteristics of the elements can reflect our emotional, psychic or spiritual states of consciousness.

Raging elements, such as storms, earthquakes, tornadoes, hurricanes, tidal waves, rampant fires, volcanic eruptions and so on, can reflect upheavals in either our outer or inner worlds.

The most common element that appears in dreams is water. Water symbolizes the unconscious, our hidden depths from which dreams draw their messages, and also the emotions. Our dreams are highly emotional.

The mystery of water is evoked in the following dream:

A lake in Canada about ten miles long, and a man and I were going along its most attractive stretch in a small boat. To my consternation and disgust I suddenly saw a great number of apartment houses built on one side of it. There were a lot of children screaming and yelling through the woods. All this made me very angry. It was such a desecration of a beautiful spot. The shape of the lake was like a human eye.[1]

The dreamer did have strong feelings against the encroachment of people into unspoiled nature. But the focal point of the dream is the eye-shaped lake. The dreamer was interested in the esoteric meaning of eyes, and saw this as a symbol for contemplation, penetration of insight, intuition and comprehension of all things. Seen from that perspective, the dream points to the need to remain calm and connected to one's inner depths despite distractions in the "landscape."

Traveling across seas and oceans and along rivers are common water themes in dreams, and symbolize the journey through life. Our "ship" can sail smooth waters, choppy waters, run into storms, and sink. Sometimes our ship may be nothing more than a dinghy.

Looking into water and seeing something below the surface can represent something within you that is becoming clear, or something that has been hidden coming into clarity.

> I'm looking over the railing of a big, cruise-sized ship, and I can see straight down into the water, very clearly. There is a lot of coral a long way down. I don't have a sense that the ship is in danger.

The ship is the dreamer's life. Coral is beauty that lives hidden beneath the surface. It is seen by looking into the depths. So, as a dream symbol, it might represent one's own hidden side, especially emotional. Other associations are that it is strong, but also fragile. It must be treated with respect and care, for it snaps under too much pressure.

The shadow side of coral is something that lies hidden from view and is an unexpected danger or threat to one's well-being or safety. However, the dreamer did not feel the negative associations applied to the meaning of her dream. She saw it as the discovery of something exotic within her.

In the following dream, a river symbolizes the direction of the dreamer's life:

> I visit L. in the hospital again. I tell her my thoughts. My message is, "When a river bed runs dry, the river has to find new channels. If it doesn't, it goes nowhere and dies."
>
> Lots of friends come and we all join hands in a circle around her bed. She jumps up to run out and get medicine, and I run after her.

L. was a friend of the dreamer's who did go to the hospital, and the dreamer visited her there. In the dream, L. is a part of the dreamer that needs healing. She comes to give herself a message that it is time to change. The river, or emotional part of her life, has gone dry. If she does not change, she will die emotionally. The friends who join in a healing circle around the bed symbolize her support system—the dreamer realized she had many friends who would give her emotional nourishment. But rather than accept the support, L. gets up and runs away, looking for medicine. The dreamer realized she was still running away from her situation, and kept looking for superficial remedies and distractions, represented by the medicine.

Diving into water, being dunked in water or bathing in water also can symbolize a baptism—a cleansing or purification signifying a fresh start, or an initiation into a new consciousness.

Drowning in water may symbolize emotional drowning, or being pulled under by emotions.

Swimming in deep water can represent doing something under your own power. If, as a swimmer, you fear unknown monsters below, there may be shadow material or a fear awaiting confrontation.

Rain often represents a significant release of pent-up emotions—think of rain as "dream tears." The amount and intensity of rain are clues to the intensity of emotions. This dream came to a woman who a year earlier had finally divorced an abusive husband to whom she had been married for nearly thirty years. As a celebration of her newfound freedom and independence, she had taken a trip to South Africa. The dream came after her return home:

I was back in South Africa walking down a tree-lined road. Suddenly it was announced that rain, once it had fallen, was to be in

the hands of the women. I felt very joyous about this as did many   213
of the people around me.

DREAMSPEAK

The dream addressed the dreamer's new life that was now free of inhibition and fear. South Africa brought to mind the emotions she experienced while there: exhilaration, freedom, new adventure, in contact with the earth, a reorientation to life. The road is a symbol of her new path in life. It is lined with trees, representing strength, vitality and endurance. "In the hands of women" meant to the dreamer something totally in control of feminine instinct: ways of living, attitudes, nurturing, and so on. In other words, the expression of her emotions were now totally her own, and did not have to be repressed to suit her ex-husband or anyone. In her marriage, she constantly had to repress and deny her own emotions. Now she was free to "rain" anytime. Since dreams often use homonyms, puns and plays on words to get messages across, she thought that "reign" also fit. She was free to reign over her life. Other people—symbols of other people in her life—were happy for her as well.

The dream carried a pleasant emotional tone that carried over into waking consciousness. It was, she observed, a healing message.

Snow and ice often represent emotions that are frozen. Walking or skiing across frozen landscapes may point to a refusal or inability to acknowledge true feelings about something—and so we try to get by on the surface.

I remember skiing down a mountain on a wide trail that was sparkling white, and was perfectly smooth so I could go quite fast. The sun was shining and the sky was peacock blue. I was going quite fast when I began to notice snakes coiled up at various places on the ski slope. My brother's voice (I got the sense he was skiing behind me) pointed out the snakes and warned me to avoid them. The snakes resembled big bull snakes—beige with black diamond and geometric patterns. They were quite obvious against the pure white background of snow. I remember speeding toward a large snake and I had to ski off the side of the slope into a deep slushy powder to avoid it. Then I woke up.

The dreamer was in therapy and coming to terms with many repressed and unresolved emotions. She tries to skim the surface (skiing fast) but runs into big snakes (healing, wisdom). She is forced to plow into emotions (the slushy powder). When she engages with the snow, it is slushy, or beginning to melt. Emotions are freeing up. Coming down the mountain is a descent of consciousness to deal with "ground level" matters.

Raging water dreams can symbolize emotional turbulence, such as in this dream:

I am standing at the edge of the shore at night. There is a huge wave of glistening white water coming in very fast toward shore. I want to run, but I seem paralyzed.

Tidal waves can symbolize being engulfed or inundated by overwhelming emotions. Such imagery might occur in the dreams of someone coping with a major loss, for example. The dreamer of this dream had lost her husband. She felt life was unraveling, and she was powerless to do anything about it.

Blizzards might indicate that a dreamer is in danger of being buried by frozen or unexpressed emotions. And tum-

bling in a flash flood or a raging river might symbolize a
sudden and major emotional upset.

Earth

After water, earth is the second most frequent element to
appear in dreams. Earth is a symbol of foundation, stability
and firmness. It also represents materiality—our posses-
sions, things and material well-being—and the body.

Dreams involving going into the earth, such as a cave or
hole, can represent withdrawal or need to withdraw to regenerate, as well as the gestation of something new. Inner
earth is a symbol of the womb. Going into the earth also
can represent going down into your own dark.

The next dream is strong on both earth and water symbolism:

*I was forced to swim down a cave half filled with water. The
water was very dirty, like sewer water, but I had to swim in it. It
wasn't as unpleasant as it sounded, I was not bothered by its
impurity. The cave had rusty red walls of stone. It led me, still swimming, to some sort of underground room, in fact a large, open-
ceilinged rusty iron box cemented onto the walls of the cave. I
pushed a little rusty iron door which used to be painted white and
I entered the room. On one side of the iron room, there were doors,
a bit like garbage disposal doors or very old oven doors. Suddenly
I had to vomit something and I deposited it on a plate I was holding
with my hands. I looked at the thing with surprise, it was a long
object very much like a piece of excrement, carrot-shaped and red-
dish brown. So I opened one of the doors, which happened to be
the opening of a garbage shaft, and I threw the thing into it. The*

shaft was so deep that the thing disappeared and I didn't even hear a noise. Then I thought I had done what needed to be done there and I started swimming back. I realized that the little iron door was closed. I thought I couldn't get out and I would certainly be drowned. But to my surprise I managed to open the door with my fingertips and, still in this dirty water, I swam to the light knowing that I was safe and I was going to get out of this. I thought I didn't mind the water being so filthy because I had something important to do in it, and I had done it.

The dream is about introspection and getting rid of unwanted garbage. When we descend into our own depths, we find it's dirty down there—lots of emotions don't get cleansed. The dreamer isn't bothered by it. We have to be willing to deal with our own "dirt" in order to change for the better.

The dreamer is forced to descend into her own depths by a relationship that doesn't move forward much, yet she is reluctant to let go of it. The situation calls for introspection and reevaluation of what she wants versus what she has. Once she is made to start this process, though, she moves under her own power (swimming).

Everything is rusty down there—we don't often peer down into our depths. Going down like this enables her to vomit up something she no longer needs and is clogging her system. In this dream, the excrement represents waste. It is dropped into the void. She manages to open the iron doors to leave, which shows inner strength and resolve. She returns to the light, or illumined thinking. The dreamer felt cleansed and purified by this dream, and also felt very clear about her situation.

Another earth symbol that makes frequent appearances in dreams is the forest. The forest is a symbol of the unconscious or the unawakened, naive or childlike self. They are dark places that can be frightening because of what lies hidden in them. In fairy tales and myth, forests are mysterious and magical, and often serve as the place where a hero's journey or adventure begins. The wandering of the hero through the forest, and the trials that beset him, represent emergence into a more conscious state or situation. It is our search for the Self.

In the legend of the Grail, one of the key figures is the young and innocent man Perceval, who grows up in a forest and then sets out to seek the Grail. In his wanderings, he is directed to the Grail Castle and enters it. There he meets the Grail King, who is languishing from a severe wound in the genitals. He cannot die from the wound and he cannot be healed until someone asks the right question. Meanwhile, his kingdom falls to waste. Perceval is not awakened enough to ask the right question. He does not even ask any questions when he witnesses a procession of the Grail.

After Perceval leaves the castle, he wants to return but cannot. He must journey and awaken more before he can return to the castle, led by a damsel, and ask the question that will heal the king: "Whom does the Grail serve?" When the question is asked, the king is healed and dies. His kingdom is restored to health.

In dreams, forests can represent an emotional or spiritual darkness in which we wander, perhaps even unaware that we are limited by boundaries. Perhaps we have a narrow perspective about something—we are unable to "see the forest for the trees."

Forests come along in dreams at times when we are changing. We find our way out of the forest of unknowing into a new awareness.

The following dream has a fairy-tale quality to it:

I found myself in a very large forest. I was walking on a path and met a beautiful young woman. I did not know her in my real life, yet I "felt" I knew her, and I can still picture her face in my mind. She was very sad. I followed her along the path and we came to a beautiful garden. In the garden to our right were two small tombstones. She told me that they were her two sons. She did not share how they died, and I did not read the tombstones, only had the sense that they were young, like between five and eight. I could tell again how sad and grieved she was, and I knew it was something she was not able to get over. I wanted to comfort her, but I did not know what to say. Behind us, to our left, was a beautiful castle, surrounded by large trees and beautiful gardens and flowers. The young woman continued on the path, and then I woke up.

The young woman is the dreamer. The tombstones of the children represent the death of her innocence in a time period related to their ages in the dream. The dreamer had suffered two losses: her father died, and she suffered public scorn over a relationship with a man. She was innocent of what others thought of her, but the damage was done nonetheless. In addition, she felt very repressed in her marriage.

The beautiful castle with its gardens represent how things used to be—or perhaps how they might yet be. A garden is a refuge, a place where one can be safe and at peace. A garden in bloom and beauty means inner growth has taken place or is occurring. (Conversely, a garden with withering or dead flowers means there are spiritual or emotional matters in need of attention.) According to Jung, trees represent the living contents of the unconscious, and can often represent the personality. The dreamer's personality thrives (the large trees and the beautiful gardens) though she does not seem to notice and continues to grieve what has been lost. But rather than go to the castle, she continues through the forest on the path.

"I was very comfortable in the forest, I loved the beauty and felt at home," noted the dreamer. "I also *knew* that the lady lived there, and lived in the castle. I have been growing, and trying to achieve an ideal self, along with what it is I want most in my outside life also."

The dreamer felt the castle represented the key to her emotional healing. Whatever she needed was right in front of her, and she didn't need to keep searching. She also realized that the path she was on—decisions she had made about her life—was taking her away from her ideals. At the time she had the dream, however, she did not feel ready to make sweeping changes in her life. But the dream bolstered her confidence in what her heart—her intuition—was telling her was right for her.

The preceding dream featured a beautiful garden, a symbol of a place of respite and peace. Tending gardens and having gardens can represent bringing something beautiful into being, or creating or having beauty and abundance in life. In the next dream, the dreamer's emotional feelings upon awakening, and her feelings about gardening, unlocked the meaning:

I was on my hands and knees planting flowers in a garden. I was all by myself.

The dreamer did not enjoy gardening work and awoke with a disgruntled feeling about the dream. The dream pointed to a job she did not wish to do alone. She had undertaken a service project that had come into flower quite nicely and was benefitting others, but had grown too time-consuming and burdensome for her to continue to do by herself. She was a self-reliant person, not inclined to ask others for help. So, she assumed more and more responsibility in silence. The dream helped her to realize that the service she was doing was good, but she should ask others involved for their help in shouldering key responsibilities.

Like forests, gardens can be magical and enchanted in dreams, too:

> I am presented with the view of a huge lyrical gate to an enchanted garden. The garden behind the very regal, stately charming gate is overgrown but powerful in meaning and beauty, a secret, wild unexplored garden, a gift to me. I feel joy and awe.

The feelings of joy and awe were so powerful that the dreamer reentered the dream in waking dreamwork. She entered the garden and saw a blond child in a white dress and crown, running. The child reminded her of drawings of fairy children by artist Salamith Wulfing.

The dream occurred thirteen days after the dreamer had returned from an enchanting and magical trip to Russia. She observed, "I think these gates looked very much like the ornate gates outside The Cathedral of the Spilled Blood in St. Petersburg. Very lyrical, fantasy, Cinderella-style gates. The garden is very overgrown with greenery all the way up to the top of the gate, but the feeling was of enchantment, of something exotic and otherworldly, and of a gift given just to me. The message seemed to be that the gates were ahead, and there for me to open and to explore, a fairy land of awe and magic. I was thrilled, excited, charmed, awed, and couldn't believe the gift ahead!"

When we face obstacles or labor toward a goal, we often

dream of going up mountains. We may drive up, walk up
or even fly up under our own power. The road or path may
suddenly change on us, becoming narrow and rocky, or dis-
appearing altogether—and we are forced to find a new
route. We might go up and down a great deal. These images
mirror situations in waking life.

Mountains also are symbols of spiritual enlightenment.
Coming down from a mountain can symbolize a reorientation to waking life, especially after a period of withdrawal.

In this dream, mountains are associated with isolation:

*I was visiting a mountain landscape from above, as from a he-
licopter. It was like a Chinese landscape, with lots of roads going
deep into the mountains. The further I was going into this landscape,
the closer to the peaks, the more I was crying and sobbing. And I
woke up crying, this time again.*

"Chinese landscape" meant "foreign" or "unknown" to
the dreamer. The images evoked feelings of aloneness: the
dreamer is all alone in her little helicopter, flying deeper
into strange territory. No one else is around, though there
are roads below—others have visited this terrain. The
dreamer was feeling intensely alone in her personal problems, crying both in and out of the dream.

Deserts can represent barrenness and bleakness, and
also places of spiritual withdrawal. In the days of early
Christianity, hermits withdrew to mountain caves to devote
themselves to a spiritual path. They became known as the
"Desert Fathers." Deserts are symbols of places of wandering and searching. The next dream is quite earthy, with a
desert, mountains and a canyon:

School is out for break. Someone takes me to a house in the desert mountains that is empty. It is a woman; she may or may not be accompanied by another person of undetermined sex. They are moving from the house, and all the furniture is out. There is a patio in the back. The sun is out and it feels good. I say, "Maybe I'll just bring a lawn chair up here and sit out in the sun." Then I worry about being there by myself. There are two dirt roads that go right by the house, intersecting. People could drive right by the house and see me all alone. Indeed, as we are standing there, two vehicles pass by. One takes the road to the left, which continues on into the desert. The other, a small pickup truck, takes the road to the right, which veers down into a steep canyon. A man with glasses is driving. The woman and I walk to the edge of that road as the truck vanishes down the road. I wonder what is down that canyon. The rocks all around me are brown.

This dream accompanied a decision by the dreamer, a novelist, to shift her work into a new arena. She no longer felt challenged by the genre she was working in. But going after a new audience would mean writing under a pseudonym and building a whole new identity. School—the work up to this point—was out, or over. The dreamer was entering a period of withdrawal (the house in the desert mountains) to gestate this artistic shift. The sun (illumination) is out and the change feels good. But things could get lonely, possibly threatening (failure in a new genre). The dreamer interpreted the woman as her intuition. The roads represent choices. The rocks are brown—everything at this point is undifferentiated. The dreamer is intuitively drawn to the choice that leads down into the canyon, or her own depths. She will have to go deep within to discover her new voice.

Earthquakes occur in dreams during times of upheaval,

when we feel we have lost our firm foundation and are suffering a shakeup. Volcano eruptions may relate to bottled-up anger threatening to explode, or a situation about to blow up. In this repeating dream, dramatic changes to earth and sky presage major changes in the dreamer's life:

It is night and I stand on a hilltop, looking up at the moon. The air is heavy, full of change. As I gaze at the moon, it begins to metamorphose right before my eyes. First, a tall conical shape appears on its top. The moon darkens and the cone glows gold/red. It looks volcanic. Then that disappears and other shapes come all over the surface—several fetal-like infants, two elephants, and a Buddha. All in a kaleidoscopic fashion. The moon also begins to descend in the sky, growing bigger as it drops. The descent whips up the earthly forces and a high wind blows. I know this is the beginning of Change, Transformation, The End and The Beginning.

I decide to run for cover. My inclination is to go toward the sea, but instead I head into the hills. I run into a cave and crawl through narrow, horizontal slits on the floor of the cave. Others have gathered in the internal chamber, but we all know we are not truly safe. I wiggle under the last slit as brilliant white light begins to flood in. "It" has descended fully. A deep and disembodied male voice begins to address us from above. I cannot remember the exact words, but they pertain to the coming Changes, why they are necessary, not all of us will survive, the reasons why those who survive will do so, and the criteria for survivors.

I know I am going to survive. I am not so much frightened as in awe. I don't know what exactly is going to happen, only that Everything As I Know It is going to change.

I wake up before the Cataclysm begins. The dream lingers and dissipates slowly. I can see the words that were spoken—they appear in my mind like italic printed script—but I can't hang on to them. I read the script, trying to remember even snippets, but as soon as I am fully conscious, they are gone.

It's tempting to interpret this dream as a prophecy for the "end times." Many cataclysm and disaster dreams had in the last years of the twentieth century were interpreted in such a manner. As I discussed in my book *Dreamwork for the Soul*, some of these dreams probably mirrored a collective swell of attention focused on doomsday prophecies concerning the turning of the millenia. But most cataclysm and disaster dreams are, like other dreams, very personal in nature and deal with circumstances in the dreamer's life.

This dream presaged a major upheaval in the dreamer's life and occurred during a time when internal pressure for change was building. It is primarily an earth dream—the firmament of the planet is going to change and there will be much destruction—but there are also elements of air (it is heavy and oppressive and a high wind blows) and spirit (the firmament of heaven shifts as well). The moon is a symbol of the feminine. Here it changes, grows a volcanic cone and comes down from the sky. The dreamer had been out of touch with her feminine, sexual side (the remote moon). It is getting ready to explode from internal pressure and come down to earth—that is, enter waking consciousness. The shapes that appear on the moon's surface herald rebirth of multiple parts of the dreamer (the fetuses); wisdom that comes from change (the elephants); and spiritual growth (the Buddha).

The dreamer decides not to take refuge in emotions (the sea) but to go within (the cave, a place of gestation). Even though the world is about to heave apart, the dreamer knows she will survive. The descent of "It" that begins with

the feminine moon brings a flood of brilliant light, which is
a positive sign of wholeness, illumination and enlightenment. The disembodied voice brings a message from the
Higher Self.

Within two years of this repeating dream, the dreamer
ended a long but defunct marriage, moved to a distant city,
changed her entire circle of friends, revamped her lifestyle
and wardrobe, and embarked on a new career. The firmament of her entire life—everything as she knew it—had
come to an end and been reborn.

Fire

Fire is a destroyer—but its destruction purifies. It razes the
old and obsolete so that new life can spring from the ashes.
Fire dreams also can represent anger, passion, sexual power
and creativity. Properly used, these things are beneficial,
even anger that is well placed. But they also can go out of
control. Fire tests us and strengthens us. Fire dreams also
occur during times of intense spiritual study, when kundalini
energy is activated.

In this dream, fire represents a dreamer's desire to eradicate what she felt was a dull life:

*My house is burning. The fire spreads to all the other houses
around it. Everyone runs out into the streets trying to escape. I'm
running, too, but the flames are catching up to me. Suddenly a mysterious man appears and carries me. I don't know if we are going to
be able to outrun the fire.*

The dreamer considered her life to be dull, and harbored a desire to be rescued from it. Not only does the fire burn her home, but everything around it. It then turns out of control and chases her, symbolizing unexpected consequences of her desire to be rid of her present circumstances. The mysterious man represents her desire to be rescued by outside forces. The message of this dream was twofold: one, if she was careless about how changes were made, then change could be far more radical or sweeping than she would like; and two, she could not rely upon someone or something else to rescue her from her circumstances.

Air

Air represents mental effort, thoughts, intellectual pursuits, logic and left-brain activities. It has a masculine energy. Air also represents freedom or escape, especially if we fly in the air. Other types of air dreams feature solving puzzles or mysteries; holding authority positions such as teacher, judge or police; being students; taking tests; and processing papers. Dreams involving organization of materials and activities (having to be somewhere on time, do a presentation, give a lecture, etc.), and riding up and down elevators also are air dreams.

I had been rushing around in the office and working all night. Suddenly it seemed that I was being examined as to my fitness for a position in a new office. The personnel manager kept pointing to a blackboard which contained an "ability test." This concerned many confusing figures with lots of ciphers and fractional divisions. The

The dreamer was an editor of a women's magazine who prided herself on her efficiency and willingness to work long hours. She detested anything to do with mathematics. She discouraged romantic relationships and was guarded in her friendships. The dream points to a lack of social preparedness. The "ability test" is conducted by the personnel manager. This was an area the dreamer preferred not to think about—represented by the unpleasant math. She considered herself socially "hopeless" and tried to be amused by that. The new office indicates a readiness or desire to push life into new territory.

A common air dream is ascending a mountain. The mountain symbolizes enlightenment, higher thinking and one's ascent in life. The ascent, or journey, is the air-related challenge.

I was somewhere where there was a very steep mountain with various roads and paths to the top. I was on my bicycle and with at least one other cyclist, a male (no one I know from present life). There may have been another cyclist, a woman. Also presently not known.

The mountain is vast and the top is a long way off. From where I am with my companions, I cannot see the summit. We were discussing what route to take. There were two automobile roads, one very direct and busy, with cars zooming up and down. The second meandered a bit, was less steep and more scenic. It was off to the side. Each auto road had footpaths alongside it. You could walk.

I looked up the mountain and at the choices of routes. If I took the side route—which it seemed I had done in the past—I could stay on my bike. If I took the direct route, it would be too steep to ride, and I would have to walk and push the bike. I explained to the male cyclist that I had usually taken the side route, which was below us, because I liked to look at the scenery. The route ran along the edge of the mountain.

He was in favor of the direct, steeper route. I looked up, and on either side of the highway were two paths, one on the left and one on the right. The left path also ran along an edge of the mountain, but seemed dangerous. It was narrow and not well defined, and I thought I could fall off. On the other hand, it might offer some scenic views. The right-hand path, on the other hand, was wider, more protected and more defined. It seemed to go straight up the mountain. I could see a small group of hikers on it. It is the obvious choice, but I do not remember making the choice, or going up the mountain. That is all I remember of the dream.

The dream came at a crossroads, change-of-life period in the dreamer's life. She was undergoing a midlife reassessment of herself. At this juncture, some people decide to pull back and coast, while others get renewed energy to push on. The dream symbolized her desire to keep on reaching for challenges, even if it meant taking the hard way up.

Turbulent air dreams involve high winds and storm systems, including tornadoes and hurricanes. Tornadoes symbolize upsetting events or situations that arise suddenly and unexpectedly, and leave things in shambles. Hurricanes are destructive as well, but one has more opportunity to get out of the way.

L. and I live in a high-rise apartment building with our apartment on the ground floor. There is a vast open space of grass around the building. We have five buffaloes and a dog for pets. I put all the animals out. A sudden storm comes up. When it is over, I go out to get the animals, but they have all disappeared. The buffaloes have left behind huge piles of droppings.

The dreamer recorded these observations:

Buffaloes are symbols of abundance and plenty. In the dream, they seem to be saying that upsets may come, but I will always have everything I need. The dog represents the chthonic guide to the realms of the unconcious. There is a theme of neglect here that has cropped up in my dreams of animals before: I neglect them and they die; in this case, they run off in the face of a storm. Here the storm seems of little significance to me—it comes up quickly, is not severe, and I am not threatened in my apartment tower. Perhaps the dream is telling me that I am too limited in my tower, and so my creativity escapes.

The buffalo droppings are gifts of the substance of creativity. Again, I have plenty around me; I am not lacking, despite my neglect. If I am going to use the excrement, I will have to go out and shovel it up myself.

I seem to be oblivious to the abundance around me—I let it out and it slips off, but leaves behind something I can use.

Other turbulent air dream themes are nuclear explosion and war. Like the earth changes dream earlier in this chapter, these images lend themselves to apocalyptic interpretations about the end of the world. However, they are more likely to deal with one's own personal world blowing up.

I get up in the morning and "know" things are different, the landscape has changed. I look out the window to see a huge black funnel on the horizon, like a cross between a nuclear mushroom cloud and a tornado. It is not nuclear, but it is poisonous, and it rains toxic particles out onto the landscape. It is spreading.

The dream dealt with a drastic change in the life of the dreamer, whose entire personal landscape was threatened by the prospect of divorce. He associated divorce with a wrecked and barren life that would be "rained on" for a long time. This change was inevitable and he felt powerless to stop it. The dream helped him to see how fear and anxiety were affecting his ability to cope with the situation.

SIXTEEN

Pursuit, Violence and Death

Dreams in which bodily harm is threatened or done to us occur throughout life. They call our attention to fears and anxieties, and to the consequences of destructive situations and behavior. We are often at war with ourselves, doing things that are not in our best interests. The Higher Self, through dreams, constantly attempts to restore equilibrium in life.

Pursuit

Pursuit dreams begin in childhood. We find ourselves being chased by dark, threatening people or scary monsters of indefinite shape. Sometimes the pursuer is sensed but never seen. We may have pursuit dreams all through life that repeat periodically. Or, we go through periods in which we frequently dream of pursuit.

Pursuit dreams deal with something that must be confronted, resolved or integrated. We avoid something, and so life goes out of balance. The pursuer tries to get our attention. Often we avoid something because we fear it, and so the pursuer takes on an air of menace or evil.

Sometimes the pursuer is our shadow. The shadow wants to be accepted and taken in. Marie-Louise von Franz, noted Jungian analyst, observed that sometimes the shadow represents something that truly is to be avoided—such as destructive tendencies of the psyche. However, she estimated that about 80 percent of what pursues us in dreams really is a valuable part of us and should be acknowledged and integrated. When we stop being afraid of pursuers, we find they are not so threatening and evil after all.

I always have dreams of men chasing me and trying to kill me. I always cleverly manage to escape and fend them off, but I always wake up from these dreams feeling exhausted, physically worn out— and, of course, a bit unnerved.

The dreamer was struggling with issues related to her sense of femininity. In her efforts to be more "feminine," she was denying her natural masculine side, her animus. It was chasing her because it could not be denied and repressed. Her unconscious fear was that to accept her masculine part of herself would mean the destruction, or death, of her feminine part. In the dreams, she feels clever to avoid the pursuers—but the effort leaves her exhausted.

The more we ignore or repress something, the more

desperate a dream pursuer is to grab our attention, and often resorts to violence. Sometimes the violence is a warning of the harm we are doing to ourselves.

I'm being pursued by a threatening man. I run as fast as I can, but he catches up with me, and pulls a knife out of his coat and stabs me in the back. I can feel the blood pouring out of me. I manage to keep running and then suddenly I collapse.

The dreamer associated this dream with a negative relationship. She and her partner engaged in hostile arguments in which she felt his words were "very cutting." She also felt betrayed (stabbed in the back) by the abusive things he said to her. The relationship was draining her emotionally and sapping her vitality (the blood). The dream warned her that she could not continue to avoid the situation (running) indefinitely. Her collapse represents the consequences.

The shadow can be represented by a pursuing animal, as we saw in chapter 10, The Animal Within. In her book *The Way of the Dream*, von Franz relates a case in which a patient of hers had recurring dreams of being chased by powerful animals. Von Franz opined that the animals represented the man's creativity, which wanted his acceptance. He had a gift for writing that he would not recognize. The patient, however, saw the animals as symbols of sexuality, despite the fact that he had satisfying relationships. One night he dreamed of being chased by a bull. He jumped a fence and the bull went up on its hind legs. When the dreamer looked back, he saw the bull's erect penis—in the shape of a ballpoint. Upon hearing the dream, von Franz commented drily, "Well, there you are." The man started writing.

A common pursuit dream is to be paralyzed and unable to move while something charges after you, or to run in agonizingly slow motion. Such images may symbolize that we are no longer able to avoid or ignore something—we literally have "run out" of options and must deal with our pursuer.

In dreamwork, ask pursuers what they represent and why they are chasing you. When confronted, many pursuers lose their menace and seem even friendly and likable. It may be advisable to work with such dreams in a therapy setting.

Violence

Violence in dreams can symbolize unpredictable and destructive situations, or inner conflict:

I'm walking along a street and pass a young man who looks kind of wild and disheveled. Just as I pass him, he pulls a gun out of his coat and starts firing wildly around him. Several persons, including myself, fall to the ground and hope we will not be hit.

The dreamer was married to a man with an unpredictable and explosive temper. He would erupt over seemingly small and innocuous matters. Over the course of time, the dreamer had lost her sense of safety and security in the relationship, and felt as though she constantly had to keep her guard up against his attacks, which often didn't make sense to her. The disheveled man who suddenly fires wildly around him was an apt image.

I had dark hair . . . I was in a police military type of group, riding on a horse. I was in the front of the group next to another male. All the group were men. I heard two of the men talking behind me, stating that I was in the group because I had proven myself. Then, we got orders to go to this town to try to stop something happening there. When we got there, it was too late, and someone set off a bomb. We knew we only had seconds to take cover, I could see myself jumping headfirst into a cement building with a pillar to my left, knowing that I would be okay. I had the bomb part of the dream twice.

The dream repeated, and the dreamer sometimes dreamed of herself as blond and sometimes as dark-haired. Light and dark in dreams can symbolize one's two natures: light is waking consciousness and dark is shadow or unconscious—things that are repressed or below the surface. A person who has dark hair in a dream—whether someone else or the dreamer—may symbolize something that is repressed.

A police officer or military figure who has "proven herself" has respect and authority. The dark-haired officer represented the dreamer's repressed desire to be respected more by others, and to be more in control of her life. Police and military are charged with controlling order, too; the dreamer was trying to maintain order in her life. She wanted to make changes but was reluctant to do so because the changes would upset others.

The bomb represents something that is about to blow up in the dreamer's life: the situations she had been reluctant to change will change of their own accord, perhaps in a violent or tumultuous way. Something that is not resolved can build up pressure and explode. A relationship or situation—perhaps the dreamer's ability to cope with a stress—may suddenly come apart. In the dream, the dreamer tries to prevent the explosion, but it goes off anyway, and she is not harmed. The dream was warning her of a potentially explosive situation in her life, so that she could take steps to defuse it.

Does violence always have a negative meaning in dreams? In this next dream, the dreamer does violence to himself in self-mutilation. He saw the dream in a positive way:

I am a painter by trade. Of late, I have been trying to become an artist, a painter of pictures. Last night I dreamed I was in a studio, painting a sunset. I used every color and shade I could think of, but it seemed I could not get the right effect.

It seemed as though I was painting a great masterpiece, but could not get the desired lifelike shades. Finally I took a knife from my pocket, opened it, and slit my clothes. Then I cut a deep gash in my chest. The blood rushed out. I took a piece of cloth, dipped it in the blood, and then smeared it over the canvas.

Within a flash, the picture became changed. It was the most beautiful sunset I had ever seen. At that moment, I awoke.[1]

Blood is a symbol of vitality, passion and the life force. The dream is telling the painter that in order to achieve artistry, he must put his own heartfelt passion into his work. Finding the center of one's being requires sacrifice—the gash in the chest. Once that is achieved, however, a magical

transformation takes place. The slitting of the clothes is the
shedding of the old painter persona.

The emotional tone of this dream is not one of anxiety or fear. The dreamer's attention is captivated by the beauty of the sunset he is able to produce after he opens his heart.

Dying and Death

I am shot in the stomach twice. I don't know who the gunman is. I fall down. I hear someone tell me I am dying.

Dreams that involve violence, dying and death are nightmarish for many people, especially when they repeat. Many people wonder if dreaming about their own death means they will die soon. People do have precognitive dreams about the impending deaths of others, but those are in a different class of dreams. So-called ordinary dreams about death and dying are not about physical death—but often they point to serious and distressing circumstances in a person's life. The dream uses the strong imagery of death to get the dreamer's attention. Notes dream expert Gayle Delaney, "a dreamer who is being killed, killing himself, or dying from disease is usually someone who is involved in self-destructive behavior or thought patterns or relationships. The people I know who have had those dreams, upon interviewing themselves, conclude that their dreams are red flags pointing to some area in their lives that is going terribly wrong."[2]

Most dreams in general call our attention to something that needs to be changed. The more dramatic the image, such as violence, dying and death, the greater the need for attention and change. We may think that we can ignore or withstand a detrimental situation. In fact, we may be in danger of dying emotionally and spiritually. Our dreams tell us so.

In the case of the preceding dream, the dreamer was being warned of the emotional consequences of staying in a bad relationship. The unknown gunman is the dreamer's refusal to face facts. The stomach and intestinal area is the vital seat of life. Being shot in the gut is fatal.

Sometimes death and dying dreams bring healing messages relating to the passing away—or need to pass away—of something no longer needed. Such things might be old beliefs or behavior patterns, or jobs we've outgrown, or relationships that no longer work. Sometimes such dreams help to prepare us for an eventual passing away of loved ones. The following dream a woman had about her husband addressed both change and preparation:

There was a muddy ditch maybe ten feet long and three feet wide, coming to a blunted point at each end. B. lay in the ditch, fully clothed and facedown at first and then face-side up. The mud clung to him, fully covering him, face, head and all.

He lay absolutely still and I pushed the thought away that he might be dead. But he looked so dead that I began to fear he was not pretending, but really was dead. Really dead?! Oh no! Very scared, I then screamed at him, "B., you are scaring me!" Still he did not move. End of dream.

The dreamer intuitively knew this was not a precognitive dream about the impending death of her husband. But she did not understand what it was trying to tell her. She presented the dream to a dreamwork group, where she had a powerful and unexpected connection to her own fear of her husband's eventual death. It was a fear very deep below the surface of her conscious awareness. "I realized B.'s death, should he predecease me, scares me because after fifty years together it would be like losing a vital part of myself," the dreamer said. "Suddenly I realized how deeply I care for him and appreciate him, and knew this would affect how I treat him."

The dreamer resolved to show her husband every day just how much she loved him. She found her behavior changing. Without effort, she was kinder and more patient to everyone, not just her husband.

"I believe my inner being (God or the Light within) gave me this dream to wake me up, make me understand, cause me to change," said the dreamer. She felt even more strongly about this meaning after doing some study of near-death experiences. She felt the dream had given her an opportunity to change before having to experience her own life review after death, in which she would see all the positive and negative things she had done.

This dream about death directly related to a fear of a loved one's death, and a need to change on the part of the dreamer. In the following examples, death themes relate to more dire, destructive situations and call attention to the urgent need to change.

DESTRUCTIVE RELATIONSHIPS

The next two dreams came to a woman who was in an abusive marriage. She knew she should get out of the relationship, but was afraid to do so. The dreams showed in a dramatic way how the abuse was killing her emotionally and spiritually.

Dream 1:

I am lying on a mat, covered, suffering from some sort of disease which causes my skin to become very thin, and I bleed through it — large, wound-like bloody patches open up. The blood oozes out rather than flows. I know it is fatal. There are one or two persons around me, plus Mom. I tell Mom I am going to die. I feel faint and am terrified of blacking out, lest it be the end, and I die. I don't feel ready to die—I don't have my spiritual house in order. I am too weak to get up.

Dream 2:

I hear that F. [a male friend] is dying of cancer—it has gone to his brain. I want to go see him, but I am afraid to. I haven't seen him for about fifteen years, and I worry that I would be unwelcome, either by him or his wife. Also, I cannot believe that he is terminally ill, and I am afraid to see him ravaged by the disease. He was so vital and handsome and only five years older than me (in reality only four years older). This fact is very hard for me to grasp, that someone I know near my own age is dying of cancer.

So instead I go to visit O. [a woman friend] in the city. We are just going to goof around and do nothing in particular. We go out on the streets and just start walking. I start telling O. about F. I still want to visit him but know she won't go along. I emphasize that I can't believe he is sick, let alone dying, especially since he is only five years older than me. O. is sobered by this age similarity.

Suddenly we are both in the hospital where F. is. It is a vast, multileveled structure, and the rooms are open like a honeycomb.

We are high up, looking down on the room where F. is supposed
to be. We are so high up that I can't see a figure in the bed. Then
a crane enters from the back of the room and starts dismantling the
bed. I realize that I've come too late—F. is dead, and they are
taking his things away to be burned.

I still can't believe it. I keep thinking of him in life. Then I berate
myself for not seeing him before he died. Surely, as he lay at the
threshold of death, appearances (physical) and old grievances
didn't matter. He would have been glad to see me, but now he is
gone forever.

I wake up feeling distressed and sad.

Most of the abuse from the dreamer's husband was verbal. If she reacted against his name-calling and criticisms,
he accused her of being "thin-skinned" and unable to take
a "joke." In the first dream, her skin is so thin that her blood,
her vitality, literally leaks out. This is the emotional toll the
abuse has taken. Her mother in the dream is her own nurturing side, her instinctual self.

In the second dream, she sees the rational part of herself, represented by a male friend, F., sicken and die of
brain cancer. She can't believe he is sick—just as she cannot
believe she is seriously suffering from her abusive relationship. The brain cancer represents what is wrong with her
thinking. Her reluctance to visit F. and confront his illness
symbolizes her reluctance to face her situation.

The next dream shows how a woman literally is being
"killed" by a relationship:

I found myself out in a body of water, possibly a lake. The water
was about chest high. There were a group of people there, two of

them were the group leaders, a lady and a man. I remember at times feeling as though I weren't part of the dream, only watching it. I did not visualize the faces of anyone in this group, except for a young attractive lady that was with, and facing, the man that was the group leader. The man had a small pistol is his hand and I knew that he was going to shoot the young lady facing him, and she knew it too, but was not afraid. He shot her three times, first in the heart, then the mouth, and then the stomach. I did not see any blood, nor did she go under the water. He simply carried her ashore. The lady group leader also shot one of the infants in the group. It was like it was supposed to happen, and it was okay. I did not notice the faces of anyone else, other than the young attractive lady. This is probably one of the strangest dreams I have had, and do not have any idea how it relates to my life. I just feel it seems odd once again, how the young lady's face is so vivid in my mind, like I "knew" her in the dream, but do not know of anyone like her in my own life. Sometimes I have the feeling that "I" am the young lady. When I share this, I feel a tightness in my heart.

Dreamwork helped the dreamer understand what the dream was showing her about her own life. She was in a stifling marriage, and felt boxed in personally, emotionally and creatively. She had decided she was not ready to change her circumstances—but her dream (and other dreams with similar themes) were trying to warn her of the consequences of allowing her soul to wither.

She acknowledged what she intuitively knew: the young woman was her. In the dream she is up to her chest (or heart) in emotion, symbolized by the water. She calmly accepts the "necessity" of being shot in three key spiritual centers: the mouth, which expresses one's true self; the heart, which knows truth; and the stomach, or gut instinct.

Her gut instinct was telling her to leave the relationship; her heart was giving her the same message; her voice yearned to express her true self. All three were being violated and "killed" by her decision to stay in the relationship. Although the man in the dream can be seen as a symbol for her repressive husband, it also is a symbol of her rational, or masculine side, which is forcing the rest of her into submission to accept the circumstances. The result of being stifled is that creativity—the expression of the true self—is killed. This is demonstrated in the dream not only by the woman being shot, but also by the woman killing the infant. Babies often symbolize something new coming into being. A new part of herself is killed before it can grow.

Besides the acceptance of this violence on the part of the dreamer in the dream, there is almost a feeling of apathy pervasive throughout it. Sometimes when we feel trapped, an emotional deadness or apathy sets in. We feel we are powerless to change things. Such dreams, however, indicate otherwise. Dreams show us what we need to heal. With that revelation comes the intuitive understanding that we have the means and the strength within us to do so.

In the next dream, the image of a vampire aptly represents the consequences of a relationship for a dreamer:

A young woman is pursued by a vampire, and finally is caught. I watch the vampire bite her on the neck and drink her blood. I am sickened. I wonder if she (the victim) is going to die.

The dreamer described the young woman in the dream as a "good girl," but not someone she knew in waking life. The young woman was, of course, herself. The vampire was a man she was dating. He was possessive and manipulative.

The relationship literally was beginning to drain the dreamer's energy and interest. She wanted to break it off, but couldn't bring herself to do so. The dream told her she was in danger of an emotional or energy "death" if she did not take action in her own interests.

DYING OR DEAD RELATIONSHIPS

I am at an airport watching big jets land. I make note of their appearances and how much noise they make. I am supposed to be meeting some people who are flying home due to someone's death. This death (of a male) was played out in an earlier dream that now I can't remember. It had to do with a large group of people who lived together in a house with a Western frontier kind of atmosphere. These people really are ghosts—the Friendship Circle—though others think they are real.

I find the people I am to meet, a couple, and take them to the house. There are wilted flowers—pink roses—everywhere either due to a party or the funeral. They unpack and give me a box of things. It isn't clear whether they know about the death or I am supposed to tell them. There is another container of boxes with some sort of secret meaning.

As I go through the items in the box they gave me, I start to eat the roses. Some taste good, but I spit out one that is particularly wilted and dry, and has an ant in it. There are pearls in one little box in the box. I am supposed to know what they mean.

The phone rings and it is Frank, the "head ghost." He tells me the other ghosts have things to do for a while, but I can summon him. Later, the Friendship Circle wants to meet with me. Just as I ask why, the phone rings for real and wakes me up.

Pink roses are a symbol of love. What is dead here is love—a marriage. There is already an unbridgeable emotional gap between the partners, symbolized by the death of a man in a distant location. Jets and airplanes are often symbols of the desire to escape—fly away from a problem or an unpleasant situation.

The dreamer eating the wilted roses represents her attempts to revivify the relationship, but an ant (something distasteful) spoils the attempt. The boxes with secret things in them represent self-discovery. The Friendship Circle of ghosts—headed by Frank, or frankness or honesty—were interpreted by the dreamer as her inner circle of intuitive guides. Intuition seems intangible to some people but real to others—and here the intuition is real to the dreamer, for she sees and interacts with the ghosts. Frankness and honesty calls on the inner line and makes himself available. The dreamer will be guided well by following her intuition.

In the following dream, a dreamer's desire for an unhappy marriage to end—but without her having to take action to end it—surfaces in a death wish about the husband:

I am in a big city with W. [husband]. He is in business dress. We are trying to cross a busy street at one terminus of a high bridge with a steel arch across the top. The light is in our favor but just about to change. W. wants to dart across, but I caution him not to, as I know that when the traffic will start up it will be merciless.

He goes anyway. The light changes and the traffic begins to zoom. W. is dodging cars while I watch in horror. He runs this way and that to avoid getting hit. Then, to avoid being struck by a semi truck trailer, he races to the side of the bridge and leaps over the railing. I scream. There is either water or concrete far below. I am certain he has jumped to his death.

For agonizing moments, I stand paralyzed and cry hysterically. Finally I realize I must call for emergency help. I run down some stairs by the bridge. Partway down the water comes into view. It is crystal clear, like a swimming pool. I see W.'s crumpled form, minus his suit jacket, on the bottom. People are standing at the water's edge looking, and someone is diving trying to rescue him. I am quickened with hope that he is not dead after all. I must run and get help.

The dream expresses an unconscious death wish. The dreamer was unhappy and wanted her situation to somehow resolve itself by *Deus ex machina*—the hand of God. In interpreting her feelings at the end of the dream, the dreamer realized that deep down inside she was terrified of the consequences of an end and wondered if she really still wanted the relationship to work. She also saw the bridge as a symbol of potential transition to something new—a way through the obstacles they faced, symbolized by the busy traffic.

NEED FOR CHANGE

My twin sister died. I was really happy about it. I felt so relieved when her coffin was being lowered into her grave.

The dreamer had no twin sister, only an older brother. The twin represents the dreamer herself. The dream reveals an intense unhappiness with her self-image. The dreamer entered therapy.

Premonitory Death Dreams

There are many cases on record of people dreaming of impending death, either of strangers (such as in a plane crash) or of people they know. These dreams are not symbolic, but previews of real events to come. Such dreams are significantly different than "ordinary" dreams; the dreamer intuitively knows this difference. They may be strangely lit with a surreal, brilliant light and seem very realistic. They usually repeat.

I dreamed I was awakened by the sound of a car pulling up outside of the house. It had a strange-sounding engine, and it kept idling. My bedroom was on the second floor. I got up and peeked out the window. It was a long white car, not a limousine, though, and very shiny. I could not see the driver, or if there were any passengers. While I was looking at it wondering about it, I saw the front door of our house open, and my brother come out. He was wearing his pajamas. He got into the car and it drove away. I had a funny feeling that I would never see him again. It was a strange dream and somehow felt "different." Everything was weirdly lit.

The feeling of unease continued after the dreamer awakened. The dreamer, a woman in her twenties, was still living at her parents' home after graduating from college. She was the oldest of four; the younger brother in the dream was fourteen. This dream repeated several times, always leaving the dreamer feeling uneasy. Within a month, the younger brother was killed in a skiing accident. The dream was very unsettling to the young woman, for in retrospect she felt she had received a premonition of her brother's death. The white car is a modern dream version of the death coach of folklore—the coach that comes to the houses where a death is imminent. The death coach is most often a funereal black, but also can be white. In folklore accounts, the driver has no face or keeps his face hidden.

The dreamer had no experience with psychic episodes, and was concerned that she was going to start having other death-warning dreams. However, this was not the case, not even when her father died several years later. Why did she have a dream warning concerning her brother? We have no way of knowing the answer why. Perhaps all the psychic and emotional conditions necessary for this type of dream to occur were right at this particular time.

In the next case, a vivid premonitory death dream occurred to an eleven-year-old girl:

I was riding on a raft down the rapids. It was so real. A dear friend of mine and a friend of my family's was on the raft with me. He fell off and I couldn't find him. I kept going down the river and I came upon a tree full of black birds, and I heard a voice saying, "Your friend won't be coming back. He's gone."

The friend died three months later. It is interesting to note that in folklore and mythology, black birds are regarded as omens of death. As the dreamer grew older, she developed psychic abilities and had other premonitory dreams. One concerned her mother:

I just remember being in a room with my mother. We had the window open and we were in a high-rise building of some sort. She was leaning over to look out the window and fell out. When I looked out the window, she was at the bottom of the street and I knew she was dead. This dream awakened me and I found myself sitting straight up in my bed talking out loud saying, "Oh, no, not my momma."

Within five months, the dreamer's mother suffered a massive heart attack and was rushed to the hospital, where she died three days later. The dreamer was in the waiting room with her family when a doctor came to break the news. She shouted, "Oh, no, not my momma!"

It is important to understand that dreams in which we or others are in danger should not automatically be viewed as precognitive warnings. The overwhelming majority of such dreams are symbolic, stress-related dreams.

Frequent dreams of violence, death and dying should get immediate professional attention. When life gets out of balance, our dreams give us warnings. If we do not heed the warnings, they become more dire. Such themes usually repeat until we get the message and take action. We cannot remain in destructive circumstances without consequences to our emotional, mental, spiritual and even physical health. A soul death saps our vitality on all levels.

SEVENTEEN

The Dead

Just two weeks after his forty-ninth birthday, Bob suffered a heart attack at 4 A.M. one morning and died. His death, completely unexpected, was a severe shock to his partner, Anne. Soon after Bob's passing, Anne had the most profound dream she had ever experienced:

We were holding each other and I felt something running down my leg. I looked and it was blood. He tried to help me wipe it away and I realized I had no skin at all. I was just raw meat. He tried to gently stroke me to help me stop bleeding. I knew that he was trying to tell me he was there for me, and although I felt totally raw, exposed and unprepared for his death, that he would help me.

The dream graphically expressed the intensity of Anne's
grief: total rawness and exposure, and a bleeding away of
vitality. Four years later, she still experienced waves of emotion just recounting the dream. Yet despite its painful imagery, the dream contained a healing balm as well:

> *To have my lover gently stroking my raw body to help soothe*
> *me, in retrospect, was a message about the work I was about to*
> *begin toward my spiritual rebirth. His death freed me from physical*
> *concerns, and the knowledge that we don't die has changed my life.*
> *Who needs skin to connect? We don't!*

Bob's death led Anne on a spiritual journey in which she
awakened her natural gifts of intuition, psychic ability and
healing. The comfort she felt in the dream gave her the
courage and energy to undertake the journey.

How and Why the Dead Appear in Dreams

Unlike dreams of death and dying, which are usually distressing, dreams of people who have passed on often bring
comfort, relief and joy. When I was working on my second
book on dreams, *Dreamwork for the Soul*, I asked people
to contribute dreams of a transformative nature. I received
more dreams about the dead than any other type of transformative dream. Clearly, our dreams of the dead have a
powerful and lasting emotional impact on us.

In grief counseling, dreams of the dead generally are
regarded as wish fulfillments and compensation in the
mourning process. We miss the person who has died or we

have unresolved business, and so we dream dreams in which they assure us that all is well.

In psychology, dreams of the dead generally are regarded as representing something in the dreamer, or something in the dead person that is important to the dreamer (such as a quality or ability).

These interpretations certainly apply to some dreams of the dead. And as we get older, it's natural that our dreams will be populated with more people who have died. However, I believe that some dreams of the dead—especially the recently dead—are true encounters, real events in another reality. Thanks to our ability to escape the limits of the physical world during sleep, we are able to briefly meet the dead in the landscape of dreams. Such dreams usually are vivid, intensely emotional and realistic experiences, so realistic that dreamers awaken certain that their dream was not an ordinary dream. What's more, heavy burdens of grief often are healed.

The ability of the dead and the living to meet in dreams is not a new idea—it has been accepted in many cultures since ancient times. Relationships, especially with family, are seen as continuing after death, with the recognition that the ancestral spirits have the ability to intervene in the lives of the living. Dream contact with the dead is seen as positive, and having a beneficial effect for both the living and the dead.

Types of Encounter Dreams

Encounter dreams with the dead fall into three main types. One is "the farewell," and occurs especially with people who are terminally ill. The dreamer dreams that the person comes to them to say good-bye. The next day, they discover that the person died the night before, or in the early morning hours (when many dreams occur). Farewell encounter dreams also happen in cases of sudden and unexpected death, such as through accident.

A second type of encounter dream is "the reassurance," in which a recently dead person appears in a dream to reassure someone that everything is all right. It is not unusual for the dead person to be restored in health and youth, and be radiant with happiness and energy.

A third type of encounter dream is "the gift." A dead person, not necessarily recently deceased, appears in a dream to impart advice, solutions to problems, or creative ideas, or to bestow blessings of love and forgiveness. The gift might simply be their visit. Sometimes a long conversation is shared, the details of which may not be remembered upon awakening.

Themes within these three types of encounter dreams are the eternal bond of love; forgiveness; blessings; assurances; gifts; and information about the Other Side.

If you have an encounter dream involving a dead person, it is important to trust your feelings and intuition about the dream. People often awaken with a certainty about what the dream means. It is important to consider such factors as mourning and wish fulfillment, but these are not the only explanations for encounter dreams.

The esteemed Scottish journalist, critic and playwright William Archer, who raised the standards of theatrical productions in England through his influence, was very interested in dreams for more than twenty-five years. The plot for his only successful play, *The Green Goddess*, came to him in a dream. For the last ten years of his life, he kept a dream diary, which he placed in his book *On Dreams*, published posthumously.

In 1918, Archer's only son, Tom, an officer in the Inns of Court Volunteers, was killed in World War I fighting. Tom's death affected him deeply, and sent him into an exploration of Spiritualism—a common reaction of the bereaved in that conflict. In 1923, Archer had what he called "the briefest, vividest, most real-seeming dream I have ever had":

> I vaguely remember other dreams preceding it, but there were no antecedent events attached, so to speak, to this. I suddenly found myself sitting in my revolving chair at the deal table in my study. Mrs. M. (my housekeeper) opened the door in great excitement and said, "It's your son, sir, come back after all" (I can hear the exact tone of her voice). Then Tom, in civilian dress, exactly as he was in life, rushed in and stood beside my chair. I held out my arms to him, but seemed somehow to be paralyzed and couldn't touch him. I thought this a natural effect of emotion, and for an appreciable time did not doubt the reality of the scene. I remember how already thoughts were running through my head as to how the news was to be broken to his mother and his wife. His face seemed to change and grow graver and, as in work, greyer; but it had in no sense faded away before the dream ended as abruptly as it had begun, in my awakening. The whole episode seemed to last, I should say, less than a minute.
>
> I had not been thinking of him more than usual, nor had anything special occurred to bring him into the foreground of my mind.[1]

This dream has the hallmarks of a farewell encounter. Most farewells occur very close to the time of death, or within a few weeks, but it is not unusual for such a dream to occur much later. They seem to happen on their own timetable, and are not dependent on our preoccupations with the dead—as Archer noted, he had not been thinking particularly about his son prior to the dream. The vivid "realness" of the dream greatly impressed Archer.

About a year and a half after this dream, Archer died following an unsuccessful operation. The dream does not have the characteristics of a precognitive death dream, but perhaps it did serve as preparation for his transition.

After the sudden death of her sister-in-law at age forty-nine, Sharon had a vivid reassurance dream about her:

M. was a person who did everything to the best of her ability. She was a very bright woman. She was passionate about many things. She was politically astute. She had been a protester against the war in Vietnam, she even broke men's legs (with their permission, of course) to keep them from being drafted. (I did not know this while she was alive—this was revealed by my brother during her eulogy.) She was a gourmet cook—the perfect hostess—putting flowers all around the house for your enjoyment during your visit. Nothing was too good for you. Educationally she had an ABD (all but dissertation) in psychology and counseled people who were in terrible condition (psychologically)—people on the streets, etc. She spearheaded a program to help abused women. She and I were not really close; however, I cared for her as a family member. She and my brother lived on the West Coast and I lived in Middle America and then in the East.

It seemed to me that both my brother and she did not have any religious practices that they adhered to. They were more concerned with the human condition. They had many friends together and individually. Although M. had a strong personality and could generate some negative feelings by her approach to you. She was so bright that I think it didn't occur to her that she could be intimidating with her knowledge and skills, or that you might not agree with her philosophically and could not express it as well as she could.

The dream: I found myself on a path in a vacant lot or field that had been mowed down. The path was well worn and dusty. I was following a person with long, flowing, rather voluminous dark hair. (This could describe my sister-in-law's hair—I never saw the face of the person I was following—but my interpretation of it was that it was my sister-in-law.) This person was walking at a fast pace. I was trying to catch up with her. We approached a house—a little white bungalow. She went in and I followed. In the house there were many ladies dressed in silken robes with turbans on their heads—the clothing was colorful, luxurious and rich looking. There was a sense of serene beauty and reverence. After looking around, I could not see the person I was following, so I went into the next room. This room was enormous (nothing at all like a room in a small bungalow). The room was more like a large hotel atrium, however it went up farther than I could see and it did not have a commercial feel. It had a solemn, peaceful, reverent feeling—there was a spiral staircase all around the edges of the room and on the different levels there were people dressed in all manner of elegant robes, men and women. I got the sense that they were holy people. I looked up at them and they looked down at me. I caught sight of the person that I was following. She was leaving the house using the back door. I followed. She quickly went down a path and into the woods. I was following her when suddenly she disappeared into the ground. This upset me terribly to see her just get quickly pulled into the earth. I began using Reiki—with my hands positioned over the ground—thinking I could sense where she was and could pull her out. Nothing happened, so I kept on trying—moving around a bit.

Suddenly there rose up out of the ground a man lying on his

back, eyes closed. He was wearing a beautiful blue velvet robe with a magnificent medallion on his chest. This surprised me—but I did not stop doing the Reiki over the ground, still hoping to find her. After a bit, I heard people around, and they were saying something to me. They were saying, "Thank you for bringing back Pir Vilayat Khan." I recognized the name as a Sufi leader or holy man. I wondered about this—but still wanted to look for her. Here the dream ended—or did not get retained in my memory.

I interpreted this dream to mean that my sister-in-law was meant to do important spiritual work in the world and would be reborn again soon. This thought has given me some comfort—as if she stopped short in this life so that she could complete a very important mission.

Even though the dreamer had no direct communication with the figure she knew was her sister-in-law, information was conveyed to her about her sister-in-law's activities and purpose as they continued on after death. The dream brought great comfort to Sharon.

Going into the earth suggests a time of incubation or gestation, a time of being out of reach. Blue appears often in dreams of a spiritual nature.

Similarly, a vivid dream brought reassurance to D.:

My mom passed away on January 7. A few nights after her burial, I had my dream. It was my mom's life. It was as if I was looking at a wallet photo album. All the pictures were wallet-size. The first photo was when Mom was a young child. It was as if someone was flipping the photos one by one. The last photo was actually the last one taken of Mom on Christmas Day. I think Mom was telling me she had lived her life full circle.

The dreamer described her reaction to the dream:

It felt like old times when I'd come for a visit and we'd look at old pictures. It was the first peaceful night's rest I'd had since Mom passed away. I really feel she wanted me to know it was time to let her go. I do remember smiling while I was viewing her life. I did not make it before she passed away (I live 1,500 miles away). I kept asking her to hold on until I got there, but she just couldn't. I don't know if that would have any impact on the dream or not.

This dream may have helped to compensate for the dreamer's inability to reach her mother before she died. Nonetheless, the realism of the dream had an immediate healing effect.

In the following dream, a deceased grandmother came in a dream at just the right time, bringing a gift of encouragement and assurance. The grandmother had cosigned for her seventeen-year-old grandson to enlist in the U.S. Marine Corps, and then died later the same day. The two had been very close—she was always a source of spiritual faith and strength during the grandson's troubled childhood. The grandson found boot camp to be grueling. During a particularly demanding period, he had this vivid and realistic dream:

My grandmother was standing at the stove, getting something out of the oven. I was standing near her, watching, and she spoke to me and said, "Everything will be all right." The peculiar thing to this dream was that it was so realistic and in the "now" as if the event were actually taking place; however, I was a young boy in the dream appearing to be about nine or ten years of age!!!

I have a vivid recollection of this dream and I've shared it with my children, who are now grown. I see the occurrence as an inspiration and comfort to me, and often recall it during troubling periods in my life.

259

DREAMSPEAK

The appearance of himself as a young boy may have added to the feeling of comfort in the dream. There is interesting symbolism involving the kitchen and oven. Both have to do with the preparation of spiritual nourishment. The time was right, for whatever was in the oven was done.

The next dream is another gift encounter, and its healing impact remained vivid for more than twenty years for Michelle, who lost her first husband to cancer when she was twenty-two:

We met in high school, fell in love, moved in together just after my fifteenth birthday and were married when I was seventeen. It was a difficult life in many aspects, having to grow up so quickly, but Chris was a natural at living and all he wanted to do was play. I wanted to play too, so we were perfect for each other. He was the love of my life.

The fun began to diminish when Chris started to get sick. At first I didn't believe him, thinking he was just making excuses not to have to go to work. On the day he threw up blood, I knew he wasn't lying anymore.

Doctors didn't believe him. Who is going to take some long-haired freaky-looking person seriously? Unfortunately, by the time the tumor was discovered, the cancer was in advanced stages.

At first I tried to take care of him at home, giving him pain shots every three hours, but it got to be too bad. He couldn't eat anymore and I watched him suffer so. After about a year and a half, I visited him in the hospital for the last time.

I requested the coffin to be closed at the funeral. He weighed less than one hundred pounds—a mere shadow of his brilliant beautiful self. I wanted everyone to remember him the way he was—not how he looked then.

For over a year after the funeral, just before I would go to sleep, I would see that closed coffin and relive the pain of his death. Every single night. It was like a permanent event, even though I tried not to think about it, I'd lay my head down and wait for the camera to start rolling the film. I thought I was going to cry every night for the rest of my life.

Then one night I had a dream. Chris came into the bedroom and stood at the foot of the bed. He reached his hand out to me and helped me out of bed. And we walked. We walked for hours. We talked about everything. Anything I wanted to know. Then we met all our friends in a circle. Those living and passed. And they all had questions for Chris. He answered them all. We laughed and joked. It was a great time.

Then it was just he and I again. And he took me to the top of a mountain. I laid facedown on the ground. He gently put his foot on my head and pointed outwards as if to give commandments to the Universe.

He said to me, "Now see . . . see like the birds see." And I did. I was seeing through the eyes of birds. I was flying through the sky. And could see myself on the ground and Chris above me directing the experience. I could see things in a much different way but in many ways the same. It was a very powerful experience.

When we were finished, Chris and I walked back to my bedroom. I turned to him and asked him to take me with him. He just smiled. Without words, I could sense that he would have liked that, but he knew the Higher Plan for the both of us, so the smile was quite appropriate. I did not make that analogy until twenty years later. After that night the funeral video no longer played in my mind before I went to sleep. Chris often comes to me now in dreams but his most *favorite way of contacting me is in the form of birds cawing three times "I Love You." And today, twenty-five years later, I really do see things in a much different way but in many ways the same.*

The dream brought not only closure to grief, but a spiritual awakening as well. For some people, such encounter dreams can have a far more profound healing effect than conventional therapy, and in far less time.

In the next case, an encounter dream brought a healing gift to a young man that helped him turn his life around:

I believe very strongly that dreams are a "gateway" between realms. I have been visited by a great-aunt and two cousins via dreams. The last and most profound one was from my seventeen-year-old cousin, who passed away of a congenital heart defect. Although we were first cousins, she was raised as if she were my little sister, because our mothers are so close. I woke up in tears, because before she left, she hugged me and filled my body with the most intense feeling of love and compassion I have ever felt.

She visited me ten months after she crossed over, and during that period prior to her visit, I was going through a deep depression and was even having suicidally obsessive thoughts. I kept asking myself why she was taken away, when she was only third from the top of the transplant list, and all of our hopes were built up. I was even on antidepressant medication that wasn't working. But after the [dream] visit, the depression never hit me like that again, and I threw the medication away. Three years later, my life has improved tremendously. I am making more [money], I moved to a less stressful area, and I have improved communications with my other family members. To me, this is proof that my cousin did indeed visit, and it was no fantasy or figment of my imagination.

When intuition tells us our experience in a dream is real, we should accept the wisdom. The experience thus has power and meaning for us.

The following dreams also were real visits for the dreamer, a woman:

> I have had two dreams about loved ones who have died. The first was my grandmother. The second was my mother-in-law. Both dreams could be described more as "visits" than dreams. What I mean is both times the women were talking to me more than they were part of a dream sequence. Both times the women were reassuring me and telling me they were with me. Both times I woke up happy and grateful that I had seen them.
>
> Both dreams were very vivid. The second time (after the one with my mother-in-law) I wrote down every detail I could remember—it was about four pages long. What struck me as odd was that I can remember thanking her for visiting me. She just smiled. She wanted me to reassure her son (my husband) that she was with him. I asked her why she didn't just visit him and she replied that she couldn't because "of the way that he dreams."

The dreamer was not certain what her mother-in-law meant by that remark. Other people who have had encounter dreams also wonder why the deceased person chose to visit them instead of someone closer. The answer seems to lie in the mystery of consciousness. Think of an encounter dream as electricity that finds the path of least resistance. There is an intended visit; the dream is "sent" to the best channel. The dreamer acknowledged that she was naturally intuitive and sensitive to the thoughts and feelings of others. She also had frequent precognitive and lucid dreams. She enjoyed dreaming because it was "sort of like enjoying a good book or a movie." Consequently, she may have been easier to reach from the Other Side.

The dreamer described characteristics of both dreams:

The dream with my mother-in-law was very different. I knew I was asleep but did not feel as if I had to try to stay asleep. I remember thinking to myself, as she was walking down the road toward me, "Oh, my gosh, that's N. I had better not try to control anything. I better just let it happen." (I did not want to wake up and miss talking to her.) The first thing I said was, "Thank you for visiting me. I miss you so much." She smiled as if she understood. We both knew I was dreaming. The strongest, clearest things were: the feel of her hands in mine (smooth and plump); the feel of her cheek against mine when I hugged her; smell; her clothes (she dressed as she had every day); her thoughts to me were very clear (she wanted me to tell my husband that everything would be all right, she was with him); her little dog. I did not hear her speak but rather it seemed her responses were thoughts that I could hear.

When I dreamed about my grandmother, it felt like the current time but, I was small. She was holding me on her lap. The dream with my mother-in-law was definitely in real time. My daughter was with me. She was her current age (nine). As a matter a fact, when I said to my mother-in-law, "This is K.," she smiled and said, "I know." In a way that made me feel as if she had been watching the whole time (she died when K. was eighteen months.)

One thing did surprise me. When she walked up she had a toddler holding her hand. I have a two-year-old, but this was not my child. At the time I was dreaming I thought it was my husband (as a child). When I woke up I remembered where I had seen the child's face.

I think it was my dad as a baby. I have seen pictures of him as a child. This upset me because he is terminally ill and I felt like this was a kind of premonition. After all, she is dead, and if my dad was with her that meant he would have to be dead too. I really didn't give this much thought until I woke up.

The entire time I was dreaming I knew I was asleep. I did not want N. to go. She did not vanish at the end. She simply went back the way she came when we were finished talking. I was left with a very good, very blessed feeling. I couldn't wait to wake up and write it down. I knew before I woke up that I would need to write all of it down.

Information About Dying

As a psychic, John Russell of Cornwall, New York, is accustomed to receiving communications from the dead, which come through in readings he gives to clients. On one occasion, a woman came through in what Russell termed an "amazing dream" to share her experience of dying:

In this dream I was giving a psychic reading to a man who had recently lost his mother, and was agonizingly bereaved. His mother was "coming through" to me from "the other side," which is a normal occurrence when I give psychic readings. I've also seen ghosts, sometimes physically solid, and she appeared to me in my dream during this reading, but her son couldn't see her. She then told me to tell him something for her, and what she related to me I've never heard expressed quite this way! She was talking about how it was for her to die, and she said, "You know how when you're driving your car, and you look down and the gas gauge is on empty, and you know you're going to run out of gas? At that moment, you have this feeling, this certainty, that you're going to run out of gas, and there's nothing you can do about it. And, you know when the car stalls and you coast it to a stop, that the only option you then have is to get out of the car and walk for help, to the nearest gas station. That's how it was when I died. I knew, with clarity and certainty, that at that moment, my 'vehicle,' my body, had 'run out of gas.' And I also realized that my only option was to exit that vehicle, and walk for help, go for help, that is . . . to make my transition. And at that moment, let me tell you that I was absolutely conscious, totally coherent, totally aware. I've never been more lucid. And at the moment of transition, I have never experienced such a feeling of total and complete peace and well-being."

The dream was very realistic, like a waking consciousness experience. It left John "pleasantly astonished." The woman's explanation of her transition made perfect sense.

Seeing the Other Side

William Archer had another vivid dream in which he found himself on the Other Side:

I dreamt I was in the other world—a world after death—but I remember very little about it, except that there was nothing spectacular or sensational about it. I saw nobody I knew there. I took from a bookcase a large green book, in which I somehow expected to find great spiritual enlightenment; but some unknown person standing by spoke of it contemptuously, saying, "We're far past that here."

Then I found a telephone and rang up Dooie, and said, "Where do you think I am? I'm in the other world. I'm not dead—I'm coming back all right—but this is the other world." I remember no more. I don't think it was a long dream. But it was one of many unconnected dreams which have left only small incoherent fragments in my memory.²

Perhaps this dream was symbolic of Archer's views that the afterlife probably wasn't the grand spiritual place portrayed in religions, but something more "down to earth," so to speak. Or, perhaps he had those views and then had a dream experience in the other realm that validated what he believed. It occurred seven years before his death.

We occasionally get glimpses of the Other Side in our dreams. These dreams complement our spiritual growth, and also may serve to awaken us to contemplation of life after death. Like our other dreams, they help us in the unfolding of our life's path.

EIGHTEEN

Pregnancy and Childbirth

With pregnancy and childbirth, life changes dramatically and permanently. For most women, bringing a new life into the world is the greatest miracle they will ever experience, and a fulfillment of their greatest accomplishment. The moment of conception initiates profound physical, mental, emotional and spiritual transformations. Dreams reflect these changes. Even men dream differently when their spouse or partner is pregnant.

Pregnancy and childbirth dreams also occur without pregnancy. Having such a dream doesn't necessarily mean you are pregnant or are about to become pregnant. Instead, the symbols relate to other things in life. These dreams will be discussed in this chapter as well.

Research shows that pregnant women dream more frequently than women who are not pregnant. Several factors explain why. Early in pregnancy, the body experiences an increase of progesterone, which contributes to an increase in drowsiness. Pregnant women—at least in early stages— sleep more. Later, as a swelling uterus makes sleep more difficult, women awake more often during the night, and thus are more likely to remember more dreams. And, pregnancy brings a natural turning inward. More attention is focused on the life growing within, the changes occurring, and the anticipated birth. Whenever we turn inward or focus our attention intensely—even for study—our recall of dreams increases.

Many women simply "know" when they've become pregnant. Their intuition is attuned to the changes in their body. Sometimes the first confirmation of pregnancy comes in a dream. Our dreams are intuitive and often tell us what's going on within the body, even before outward signs develop.

I get a telephone call. A male voice announces he is "from the center" and has called to tell me I am pregnant.

The dreamer was not trying to get pregnant, but she and her husband had agreed that if she did, it would be good. Telephone calls often represent a connection to the intuition. The voice "from the center" has authority and can be seen as a symbol of "from the center of being," that is, the womb. Though the sex of the baby was not mentioned, the dreamer awakened "knowing" she was indeed pregnant and was going to have a boy. She was, and she did.

This dream was determined to have occurred the night after conception:

I'm in a house (unfamiliar) talking to B. [a friend] on a small cell phone when a big tornado hits the house, directly—I tell this to her and drop the cell phone.

The small cell phone is symbolic of the embryonic new growth. The unfamiliar house heralds the change in life. The big tornado reflects normal anxieties about how life will change and whether or not the dreamer will be able to cope with them.

Themes and symbols in pregnancy dreams change as the pregnancy progresses. Many women are surprised to discover that the contents of their pregnancy dreams are shared by other women.

Dreams That Characterize Each Trimester

FIRST TRIMESTER

During the first trimester, a woman may have lots of dreams involving water, swimming, gardens, fruit, flowers, new construction, small buildings, small aquatic animals such as little fish and tadpoles, and easy childbirth, such as babies who pop out without labor, sometimes full-grown. She may also dream of intruders in her house (the baby growing within her body), new and expanding houses (change in lifestyle), and windows (symbols of windows into the body).

This dream took place during the first week after conception:

I'm playing in a vast river; other grad students are there. It's very deep. S. D. comments on colors you can see if you dive. I jump in feet first and sink rapidly. Beautiful layers of colors, but I don't focus on them. I'm going fast and it's hard to slow—but I do, and I kick up and go up fast until I finally emerge. B. T. tells me it's better to dive headfirst—easier to turn around.

Then we are up in the treetops above the river, quite high. You can see seals and sea lions and people—all small.

The beauty of the new life lies deep below the surface of the water. The dreamer is getting accustomed to the idea of being pregnant, as symbolized by the friend's advice to dive in headfirst. The small seals, sea lions and people are symbols of the tiny growth in the womb.

The next dream features small creatures and an intrusive man:

We go to a castle. There is a big vat of "tadpoles," and they look more like lizards with big heads with a mauve pattern. They bite me, first once, then a second time, on the wrist, it won't let go, I have to hit it to get it off, no one will help me. Later a man fights me. I go to punch him, I hit the wall by my bed with my hand and wake myself up.[1]

The big-headed lizards reminded the dreamer of sperm. She had indeed been "bitten," or impregnated. She was experiencing mixed feelings of happiness at being pregnant, and of anger at being "had" by a man, how her body had been "taken over," and her symptoms of fatigue, morning sickness, and "feeling suddenly immobilized."

In this first-trimester dream, the new and different house—so different it is in another state (or state of being), represents anticipation about the change in life a baby will bring:

> *Our house is different and seems to be in [another state]. S. [husband] has rearranged it so there are three rooms for the living room instead of one. One tiny one at the back, two larger middle and front. Darker now, though. Basement steps leading down in the middle one. I like it, except for being darker.*

The living room is now three rooms in one, reminiscent of the fairy tale characters Papa Bear, Mama Bear and Baby Bear. The smallest room at the back is the baby. The increased darkness symbolizes uncertainty. No matter how much you read and prepare for your first child, you still don't know exactly how life will change when it arrives. The dreamer is pleased with the new arrangement, however. The steps leading to the basement from the middle room (the mother) indicate a turning inward.

Early feelings about the ease of caring for a baby may be romanticized:

> *I have a little girl, maybe two. I carry her up on my hip while I'm doing things, like laundry. S. [husband] is around.*

This dream at ten weeks reflects hopes for an easy delivery, and mild anxieties about caregiving ability:

> *I'm taking care of a cute baby—mine. Looks a lot like A. Big sunny room, but unfamiliar. It seems I don't know what to do next, although the baby is content and not crying. A nurse tells me I*

should be giving baby vitamins—folic acid. I haven't been, so I worry about that.

SECOND TRIMESTER

In the second trimester, dreams shift. A woman's enlarging belly brings anxieties about her attractiveness and appeal. There may be dreams about rekindled affairs with old lovers, or the husband or partner being disinterested and perhaps sexually involved with someone else. Buildings and animals are larger. There may be fewer aquatic animals and more small furry and cuddly animals, such as puppies, kittens and chicks. Women also dream of their husbands or partners and their own mothers being either a help or hindrance. There may be an increase in anxieties about caregiving and worries that the baby will "come out all right."

This dream occurred just at the beginning of the second trimester:

I go into labor and have a baby before I know it, at home. A boy, with a funny, multicolored leg. I go to call the maternity center to tell them. Then I notice the baby is sick, high fever and all. I'm not sure what to do.

Mean to call people to tell them the news, but keep putting it off.

It is not unusual to dream of giving birth to an animal, or part-human part-animal, or some other strange creature, as in this dream, which occurred at nineteen weeks:

Our new baby is a Furby, and a naughty one, very mischievous. It keeps running off and getting into small spaces, heedless of danger. I catch it and scold and threaten, but to no avail.

Many pregnant women become unduly concerned with their "distorted" body shape as the baby grows. Even women who plan their pregnancies often are surprised by their own negative feelings about their body as it changes shape. In their dreams they compare themselves to slim friends and endlessly try on clothes trying to find ones that fit.

I attend ballet class with the same instructor I had as a kid. She hasn't changed a bit. I find I can't follow along very well, and can't even do some of the stretches. She comes over and counts vertebrae and says, "Oh, yes." I know my pregnancy is why I can't do stretches.

I'm getting bigger, showing more. I try on some clothes.

Women also dream of not being able to do things because of their size:

I'm in a swimming pool trying to do water-walking because freestyle is really hard (because I'm pregnant), although it gets easier.

Dreams of cars, trucks, boats and oversized vehicles also reinforce body-anxiety issues.

Demonic or nasty children raise fears of inadequacy as a parent (as in the Furby dream), and evil intruders can represent conflicting emotions about becoming a parent.

During this period, dreams of losing the baby or not caring for it properly are common. Women dream of misplacing their babies and finding them in grocery sacks, laundry baskets, washing machines and drawers. They also dream of mishaps, such as through their carelessness, that threaten or damage the baby:

> *Our very small (five or six inches) baby is born! Not really baby-shaped—more adultlike—but definitely a baby. Happened without any labor to speak of. I am in the back bedroom and ask S. to put up the sides of the crib. I put the baby in, and he (it's a boy) gets tangled in the bedding and falls out. I hurry over to untangle him. He stopped breathing momentarily and now I worry about brain damage.*

The image of the impossibly tiny but adultlike baby who comes with virtually no labor relates to fears about labor and the uncertainties of dealing with an infant.

Child educator Patricia Maybruck recounts the following nightmare in her book *Pregnancy & Dreams*:

> *Dreamed I was at the meat counter in the supermarket. A clerk, who looked exactly like my obstetrician, invited me to come around behind the counter to pick out what I wanted. We went into this refrigerated room where all kinds of carcasses were hanging. I felt horrified at this bloody sight. On one side was a string of small ones. I asked what they were and he grinned and said, "Those are the human babies that were defective or dead. They're delicious but we usually don't tell the customers what they are. Want to try one?" I felt scared and sick (and woke up really terrified).[2]*

Several days prior to the dream, the dreamer had undergone an amniocentesis that showed she had a normal fetus. But she continued to worry that the test was wrong, or somehow would cause her to miscarry. Her fears were irrational, and were expressed in the nightmare. Maybruck helped her deal with these fears through the creation of positive daydreams and affirmations. After eighteen hours of labor, monitors showed the baby was in distress, and the dreamer had a C section. Her boy was normal and healthy. The dreamer acknowledged that she had not practiced her relaxation techniques or positive daydreams, and experienced difficulty relaxing during labor.

Nightmares about lost and misplaced babies, misshapen babies, accidents with babies and inability to care for babies are truly frightening. Constructive dreamwork can help take the terror out of these dreams.

Some women worry that these troubling dreams are premonitory warnings about dreadful things that will happen. A tiny minority of dreams do forecast miscarriages and stillbirths, but the overwhelming majority of such dreams are reflections of anxieties on the part of the mother-to-be, especially if it is her first child. Every prospective new parent worries about the health and safety of their child, and their ability to care for it and protect it. According to psychologist and dream researcher Patricia Garfield, "Most pregnant women have alarming nightmares that prove totally unfounded."[3] In fact, such anxiety dreams can prove beneficial by helping the dreamer and her partner face and deal with natural fears.

Some examples of premonitory dreams on record are babies who wave good-bye and sail off on a river of blood; dreamers who find themselves in a bath where the water turns to blood; babies found in refrigerators; and announcements by strangers that there will be no baby. It is important to realize, however, that these same images can occur in the dreams of women who eventually bear healthy children. Other factors usually involved in premonitory dreams are a "heavy" atmosphere; intense feelings of being real; disturbed emotions in the dream and upon awakening; and an intuitive "knowing." It is especially helpful for pregnant women to discuss their dreams and anxieties during the course of pregnancy, either with a therapist or in a support group.

Toward the transition from second to third trimester, women often review their own relationships with their mothers as they step into the role of motherhood. Dreams about fathers are less common. Such dreams remind the dreamer of how she viewed her parents when she was a small child, and also show the emotional need for a parent's support. Some dreams may reveal worries that the dreamer's mother will be too intrusive or controlling once the baby arrives.

I'm busy at the office. I'm very big—the baby is going to come any day. I start to go into labor. My mother comes by and announces she will go to the hospital and have the baby for me.

Many women try to juggle career and home life, or at least keep working as long as they can prior to birth. This dream reflected the dreamer's fears that she could not manage both work and family, and also that her mother would interfere in childrearing.

Dreams in which the husband is helpful or hindering occur at this stage, too. Sometimes dreams painfully show the true state of a marriage. A woman in a troubled marriage may harbor the notion (even unconsciously) that a child will improve things by uniting the parents to a cause and responsibility. The addition of children can be stressful to even the strongest of marriages, however. In her ground-breaking study, *The Dream Worlds of Pregnancy*, researcher Eileen Stukane tells of a pregnant woman who had a dream about Elizabeth Taylor and Richard Burton—a celebrity couple renowned for their bickering and fighting. The dream pointed to a marital crisis in the dreamer's life. "Dreams are known to reveal truths you may be trying to hide from yourself," said Stukane.[4]

THIRD TRIMESTER

In the third trimester, the baby becomes more "real." Women dream of its sex, appearance and name. They dream of seeing the baby through their transparent wombs, communicating with the baby, and participating in rituals (a symbol of birth). They may star in their own dramas and find people applauding and congratulating them for their "production." Delivery-fear dreams are common, as in this dream:

S. [husband] and I go to the maternity center. Their three regular rooms are full, so a woman tells us to go to another room, the "backup." She's the one who "donated" it. We check the others out of disappointment, and they do seem to be occupied with women's things. So we go to the other room, make up a bed and sit on it. I feel sheepish at this point because I'm not really in labor. Just very anxious. When the midwife comes in I tell her this. She's very nice about it, but does tell us to come to the special classes. She has misinterpreted what I am anxious about.

In the next dream, a woman gives birth in bizarre conditions reminiscent of medieval torture:

I see an image, sort of like watching a movie, of a woman giving birth. Somehow, she is suspended in midair, it seems, upright. The baby just pops right out! At the same time a piece of feces falls out as well. I think to myself that now I see why hospitals give enemas.

The feces is an interesting symbol of production of something from within the dreamer's own body or self.

Body-image anxiety dreams continue as well:

I am downstairs with a bunch of older women. One is leading them in exercise, yoga. I do my own thing—back exercises—partly because I can't keep up the pace, being pregnant, and partly because my back does hurt.

Women may also dream about traveling in vehicles at high speed, sometimes out of control; getting lost (fear of the unknown); large structures and animals; and about being touched by others, having their babies touched by others, and touching their babies themselves.

I'm in [a baby store] looking around, thinking of what we need, and pass these huge racks of discount maternity clothes. I start looking through them. I remember a red-and-white V-top that is too small, and other tops. It gets crowded with people. One woman, as she walks past me, puts her hand on my stomach, which really angers me, and I snap at her. She laughs and walks on. I yell after her, "You could at least ask first!"

Although each trimester is marked by certain dominant themes and images, any of these dreams—as well as others—can occur at any stage of pregnancy. Paying attention to dreams during pregnancy will help the dreamer see pat-

terns that point to conflicting emotions, unresolved worries, 279
and tensions in relationships.

DREAMSPEAK

BENEFITS OF DREAM ACTION

Research by Maybruck and others has shown that women who take action to resolve troubling situations in dreams are less likely to experience long labor (eleven hours or more). In *Women's Bodies, Women's Dreams*, Patricia Garfield gives this example:

I go into labor. I'm walking around the living room and I feel the baby's head come out. I reach down and pull it out—it's a little girl. The head is flesh and skin, but the body is just bones.

I'm worried. "This is not right." I blow on the baby or breathe on her, and she fills out to normal-looking. I'm still kind of concerned she will stay okay when I wake.[5]

Breath is a symbol of life and the life force, and breathing on the baby infuses it with new life. The dreamer subsequently delivered a girl, her first child, after a labor of only six hours. Garfield stresses the importance of self-programming prior to sleep with instructions not to be victimized by a nightmare, but to take assertive action. "Taking charge, having confidence in herself, and being in command may help a woman to cope with the job of giving birth to a child," she said.[6]

Maybruck found that women who confronted unpleasant or terrifying dreams early in their pregnancies experienced more happy dreams as they neared their due date. Pleasant dreams also can be induced by affirming prior to sleep that dreams will be happy.

ROSEMARY ELLEN GUILEY

The spotlight may be on mothers during pregnancy, but fathers are not left out of pregnancy dreams. Like mothers, they experience a change in dream themes and symbols. In a ground-breaking study done in the 1980s, adult and child psychologist Alan B. Siegel examined the dreams of expectant fathers. They also experience an increase in water dreams; their partners giving birth to small animals; anxiety dreams about the health and normalcy of the baby; conflicting emotions about the baby; precocious adultlike babies; appearance and name of baby; awareness of the changing body shape of the mother; love affairs with old lovers or seduction by a stranger; and worries about caregiving ability. Men also dream of giving birth themselves, with babies emerging from armpits, anuses, mouths and so on. Some of these dreams may be part of the "couvade syndrome," in which men mimic physical symptoms of pregnancy as a way of identifying with and participating in the birth process. A significant difference in the dreams of expectant fathers are themes of being left out and excluded. While women dream that they may no longer be sexually appealing to their partner, men dream about anxieties over their sexual powers and their masculinity, which they seek to redefine in a new role as father. Sex naturally decreases during pregnancy, and men can feel needy and jealous about being replaced as the primary object of a partner's attention:

I am being approached by a voluptuous woman. I can tell she wants to seduce me and I am very tempted. All of a sudden, I know I am in trouble. An alarm goes off and I think it's my watch, but when I look I realize the alarm is on my wedding ring and I have to get home to my wife.[7]

The dreamer felt the dream related to his sexual neediness, and to a need for care and attention from his preoccupied wife. He had been having a lot of sexual fantasies. The dream alarm awakened him from his neediness and stimulated him to focus instead on improving relations with his wife.

According to Siegel, a dramatic feature of men's dreams during pregnancy is the party or celebration, especially birthday parties:

I am watching people all around me dance and play. I am not seen or heard. A group comes near me and all play ceases. This group seems to have control over all. I like them. Their energy is high and has a calming effect on me. They come over to me, surround me. One of them comes over to me and gives me a bundle. It is a baby.[8]

The dreamer had been feeling very left out of the pregnancy and alienated from his wife. The dream tells him that he has worked out those feelings, said Siegel, and was now excited and ready for fatherhood.

Like expectant mothers, expectant fathers also stand to benefit by tracking and working with their dreams throughout a pregnancy. Understanding the messages in these dreams has a positive influence on the equal involvement of both partners in preparing for this significant life change.

Pregnancy, Childbirth and Babies in Non-Pregnancy Dreams

Pregnancy and childbirth dreams can occur at any time in life, especially to women. They may be particularly puzzling to women who know they are not pregnant or who are beyond child-bearing age. Many young women make the automatic assumption that such dreams mean they soon will be pregnant. As mentioned earlier, dreams can forecast pregnancies, but these symbols in dreams often relate to something else in life.

Pregnancy and childbirth are powerful symbols of bringing something new into one's life. They can occur at times of major transition, especially if there has been a "gestation" period of inner withdrawal, contemplation, or preparation. Fetuses and babies are powerful attention-grabbers, and may summon the dreamer to shift focus:

I'm at an amusement park having a good time. Suddenly I look down and see that I am holding a baby, and I realize it's mine!

The dreamer, who had no children, was shocked by this dream. The baby represents a new focus seeking her attention. In dreamwork, she realized it addressed her career path. She was working in a job that was fun and not demanding (the amusement park), but which did not utilize all of her skills and talents, and offered little chance for advancement. She had been content to "play" at an easy job—but was getting the message to do something new.

Pregnancy and babies also relate to creativity and ideas, such as in the following dream:

I repeatedly dream that I again have a little baby and I feel all the old tenderness again—or rather more than that, for all the feelings in a dream are intensified.[9]

The dreamer, a writer with no children, related the baby to her projects, and to the satisfaction of bringing a project to successful fruition.

Pregnancy dreams also can reflect anticipation about something that will happen. Infants and small children can symbolize our ability to be new and fresh, and to be able to discover ourselves anew.

For More Information About Dreams

Visionary Living
http://www.visionaryliving.com
Author Rosemary Ellen Guiley's Web site features articles on
dreams, and information about her dream workshops, books
and tapes.
E-mail: rosemary@visionaryliving.com

Association for the Study of Dreams
http://www.asdreams.org
The ASD is a nonprofit, international, multidisciplinary organization dedicated to the pure and applied investigation of
dreams and dreaming. The Web site has information on
member benefits, activities, books and articles.
E-mail: asdreams@aol.com

Dream Network

Quarterly magazine of articles and information on dream resources

http://www.DreamNetwork.net

E-mail: *dreams@lasal.net*

Or contact Dream Network at:

1337 Powerhouse Lane, Suite 22

PO Box 1026

Moab, UT 84532-1026

(435) 259-5936

ENDNOTES

Chapter 3: Flying and Falling

1. Mary Arnold-Forster, *Studies in Dreams* (New York: Macmillan, 1921), pp. 38–39.
2. Anthony Shafton, *Dream Reader: Contemporary Approaches to the Understanding of Dreams* (Albany, NY: State University of New York, 1995), p. 443.
3. Arnold-Foster, op. cit., p. 40.
4. Ibid., p. 43.

Chapter 5: Clothing and Nudity

1. Jean Dalby Clift and Wallace B. Clift, *Symbols of Transformation in Dreams* (New York: Crossroad, 1989), pp. 57–58.
2. Clement Wood, *Dreams: Their Meaning and Practical Application* (New York: Greenberg, 1931), p. 53.

Chapter 6: Sex, Marriage and Weddings

1. Wood, op. cit., p. 225.
2. Frederick Pierce, *Dreams and Personality* (New York: D. Appleton and Co., 1931), p. 264.

Chapter 7: Money, Valuables and Treasure

1. Wood, op. cit., p. 16.
2. Ibid., p. 4.

Chapter 8: Other People

1. Pierce, op. cit., p. 197.
2. Ibid., p. 154.
3. Ibid., p. 51.
4. Ibid., p. 63.
5. Ibid., pp. 63–64.
6. Ibid., pp. 64–65.

Chapter 9: Celebrities and Famous People from History and Literature

1. Pierce, op. cit., p. 74.
2. Wood, op. cit., p. 156.
3. William Archer, *On Dreams*. Edited by Theodore Bester-man (London: Methuen & Co., Ltd., 1935), pp. 164–65.
4. Pierce, op. cit., p. 139.

Chapter 10: The Animal Within

1. Wood, op. cit., p. 25.
2. Ibid., p. 95.

Chapter 11: Insects

1. James Hillman, "Going Bugs," *Spring: A Journal of Archetype and Culture*, 1988, p. 49.
2. Ibid., p. 52.

Chapter 12: Food and Eating

1. Peter Bishop, *The Greening of Psychology: The Vegetable World in Myth, Dream, and Healing* (Dallas: Spring Publications, 1990), p. 106.
2. Ibid., p. 109.

Chapter 13: Houses, Buildings and Structures

1. Pierce, op. cit., p. 50.
2. Ibid., p. 302.

Chapter 14: Transportation and Traffic
1. Pierce, op. cit., p. 48.
2. Archer, op. cit., p. 199.
3. Pierce, op. cit., p. 154.
4. Ibid., p. 227.

Chapter 15: Landscapes and the Elements
1. Pierce, op. cit., p. 263.

Chapter 16: Pursuit, Violence and Death
1. Wood, op. cit., p. 164.
2. Gayle Delaney, *In Your Dreams* (San Francisco: Harper-SanFrancisco, 1997), pp. 93–94.

Chapter 17: The Dead
1. Archer, op. cit., p. 212.
2. Ibid., p. 148.

Chapter 18: Pregnancy and Childbirth
1. Lucy Goodison, *The Dreams of Women: Exploring and Interpreting Women's Dreams* (New York: Berkley Books, 1997), p. 191.
2. Patricia Maybruck, *Pregnancy & Dreams* (Los Angeles: Jeremy P. Tarcher, 1989), pp. 185–86.
3. Patricia Garfield, *Women's Bodies, Women's Dreams* (New York: Ballantine Books, 1988), p. 174.
4. Eileen Stukane, *The Dream Worlds of Pregnancy* (Barrytown, NY: Station Hill Press, 1985, 1994), p. 87.
5. Garfield, op. cit., p. 204.
6. Ibid.
7. Alan B. Siegel, *Dreams That Can Change Your Life* (Los Angeles: Jeremy P. Tarcher, 1990), p. 89.
8. Ibid., p. 93.
9. Garfield, op. cit., p. 208.

BIBLIOGRAPHY

Archer, William. *On Dreams*. Edited by Theodore Besterman. London: Methuen & Co., Ltd., 1935.

Arnold-Forster, Mary. *Studies in Dreams*. New York: Macmillan, 1921.

Barrett, Deirdre, ed., *Trauma and Dreams*. Cambridge, Mass.: Harvard University Press, 1996.

Baylis, Janice Hinshaw. *Sex, Symbols & Dreams*. Seal Beach, Calif.: Sun, Man, Moon, Inc., 1997.

Bishop, Peter. *The Greening of Psychology: The Vegetable World in Myth, Dream, and Healing*. Dallas: Spring Publications, 1990.

Boa, Fraser. *The Way of the Dream: Conversations on Jungian Dream Interpretation with Marie-Louise von Franz*. Boston: Shambhala, 1994.

Bulkeley, Kelly. *An Introduction to the Psychology of Dreaming*. Westport, Conn.: Praeger, 1997.

———. *Transforming Dreams: Learning Spiritual Lessons from the Dreams You Never Forget*. New York: John Wiley & Sons, 2000.

Clift, Jean Dalby and Wallace B. Clift. *The Hero Journey in Dreams*. New York: Crossroad, 1988.

———. *Symbols of Transformation in Dreams*. New York: Crossroad, 1989.

BIBLIOGRAPHY

Delaney, Gayle. *Sexual Dreams: Why We Have Them, What They Mean*. New York: Fawcett Columbine, 1994.

———. *In Your Dreams*. San Francisco: HarperSanFrancisco, 1997.

———. *All About Dreams*. San Francisco: HarperSanFrancisco, 1998.

Dieckmann, Hans. *Twice-Told Tales: The Psychological Use of Fairy Tales*. Wilmette, Ill.: Chiron Publications, 1986.

Ellis, Havelock. *The World of Dreams*. Boston: Houghton Mifflin Co., 1926.

Garfield, Patricia. *Women's Bodies, Women's Dreams*. New York: Ballantine Books, 1988.

———. *The Dream Messenger*. New York: Simon & Schuster, 1997.

Goodison, Lucy. *The Dreams of Women: Exploring and Interpreting Women's Dreams*. New York: Berkley Books, 1997.

Guiley, Rosemary Ellen. *The Encyclopedia of Dreams: Symbols and Interpretations*. New York: Crossroad, 1992; Berkley, 1995.

———. *Dreamwork for the Soul*. New York: Berkley Books, 1998.

Hillman, James, "Going Bugs," *Spring: A Journal of Archetype and Culture*, 1988, pp. 40–72.

Jung, C. G. *The Archetypes and the Collective Unconscious*. Princeton: Princeton University Press, 1968.

———. *Man and His Symbols*. New York: Anchor Press/Doubleday, 1988.

———. *Dreams*. From *The Collected Works of C. G. Jung*, Vols. 4, 8, 12 and 16. Princeton: Princeton University Press, 1974.

Mallon, Brenda. *Dreams, Counselling and Healing*. Dublin: Gill & Macmillan, 2000.

Maybruck, Patricia. *Pregnancy & Dreams*. Los Angeles: Jeremy P. Tarcher, 1989.

Pierce, Frederick. *Dreams and Personality*. New York: D. Appleton and Co., 1931.

Shafton, Anthony. *Dream Reader: Contemporary Approaches to the Understanding of Dreams*. Albany, NY: State University of New York, 1995.

Siegel, Alan B. *Dreams That Can Change Your Life*. Los Angeles: Jeremy P. Tarcher, 1990.

Stukane, Eileen. *The Dream Worlds of Pregnancy*. Barrytown, NY: Station Hill Press, 1985, 1994.

Van de Castle, Robert L. *Our Dreaming Mind*. New York: Ballantine Books, 1994.

Von Franz, Marie-Louise. *Shadow and Evil in Fairytales*. Dallas: Spring Publications, 1974.

———. *Dreams*. Boston & London: Shambhala, 1991.

Walsh, William S. *The Psychology of Dreams*. New York: Dodd, Mead & Co., 1920.

Whitmont, Edward C. & Sylvia Brinton Perera. *Dreams, A Portal to the Source*. London: Routledge, 1990.

Wood, Clement. *Dreams: Their Meaning and Practical Application*. New York: Greenberg, 1931.

ABOUT THE AUTHOR

Rosemary Ellen Guiley, Ph.D., is a bestselling author, columnist and presenter. Her work is devoted to helping others achieve their goals and find fulfillment in life, creativity and work through "visionary living." She is president of her own company, **Visionary Living, Inc.**, through which she produces and markets self-help resources and presentations, especially on dreams and intuition.

Her other books on dreams are *The Encyclopedia of Dreams: Symbols and Interpretations*, a bestselling guide to understanding dreams, and *Dreamwork for the Soul*, a ground-breaking book about the spiritual and transpersonal aspects of dreams. Dreams are featured in *Breakthrough Intuition*, a comprehensive guide to developing intuitive skills. All three are published by Berkley Books.

Ms. Guiley has authored more than twenty-five books on other subjects, including prayer, mysticism and mystical experience, saints, angels, ghosts, sacred sites, and more. Her work has been translated into twelve languages, selected by major book clubs, and cited for excellence.

Ms. Guiley lives with her husband, Tom, in Arnold, Maryland.